PUFFIN B

Extreme Expeditions
THE BIG FREEZE

... as Mawson peered over the dangerous edge
of the crevasse into the icy nothingness, he
could see no sign of his colleague. About 40
metres down, an injured dog was lying on a
ledge, whimpering in fear and pain. Terrified,
Mawson called his friend's name, but no answer
came back. The crevasse was so deep he could
not even see its bottom ...

Another book by C. J. Charley

Extreme Expeditions: Conquering the World

Catherine Charley is a writer and teacher who has travelled all over the world. Her experiences include paddling a canoe down a river full of crocodiles and piranha in Peru, white-water rafting in Australia and journeying through north-eastern China in freezing temperatures of –30°c. In between, she worked for Raleigh International and learnt how to parachute and to sail.

C. J. Charley

THE BIG FREEZE

EXTREME EXPEDITIONS

PUFFIN BOOKS

To Charley, Rebecca and Dominic

PUFFIN BOOKS

Published by the Penguin Group
Penguin Books Ltd, 27 Wrights Lane, London W8 5TZ, England
Penguin Putnam Inc., 375 Hudson Street, New York, New York 10014, USA
Penguin Books Australia Ltd, Ringwood, Victoria, Australia
Penguin Books Canada Ltd, 10 Alcorn Avenue, Toronto, Ontario, Canada M4V 3B2
Penguin Books (NZ) Ltd, Private Bag 102902, NSMC, Auckland, New Zealand

On the World Wide Web at: www.penguin.com

Penguin Books Ltd, Registered Offices: Harmondsworth, Middlesex, England

First published 2000
1 3 5 7 9 10 8 6 4 2

Set in 11pt Futura Book

Made and printed in England by Clays Ltd, St Ives plc

British Library Cataloguing in Publication Data
A CIP catalogue record for this book is available from the British Library

ISBN 0–141–30345–X

Contents

'GREAT GOD! THIS IS AN AWFUL PLACE...'

The words of the explorer, Captain Scott, when he and his men finally reached the South Pole on 17 January 1912 after weeks of terrible hardship. In the tough days that followed, as they tried to struggle back to the safety of their base hut, Scott lost two of his men in the most awful conditions.

Later, trapped in his tent by a howling blizzard, Scott had to accept that he and the remaining two men were facing death themselves. He continued his diary as best he could: '... we are getting weaker, of course, and the end cannot be far.'

Months later, their frozen bodies were found.

Why and how did Scott's team come to be in this 'awful place'? To find out we need to go back to the beginning, to discover the reasons why the Poles have been one of the greatest and most extreme challenges to humankind.

EXPLORERS TALK ABOUT THEIR EXTREME EXPEDITIONS

'A few toes were not much to give to achieve the Pole.'
Robert Peary, after losing eight of his toes on his first attempt to reach the North Pole in 1898.

'The Arctic sounds like a train shunting yard. There is a surprising amount of loud noise almost all the time, lots of creaking and cracking, as the ice shuttles around and falls off.'
Claire Fletcher, member of an all-female relay team to the North Pole in 1997.

'And there were Polar bears! Everyone had to carry a gun, and I had never even touched one!'
Mike Stroud, as he set off (with Sir Ranulph Fiennes) to make an unsupported expedition to the North Pole in 1986.

'I am just going outside and may be some time.'
Captain 'Titus' Oates, just before he went out into a blizzard to die so he wouldn't hold back his colleagues, 17 March 1912.

2

'The ice was as solid as concrete.'
David Scott-Cowper, solo sailor in the North-west Passage, stuck with his boat in pack-ice in 1986.

'You don't go to the North Pole and not expect to have a hard time.'
David Mitchell, part of an expedition in 1997 to be the first men to walk from Siberia to Canada via the North Pole.

'Take it all in all, I do not believe anybody on earth has a worse time than an Emperor penguin.'
Apsley Cherry-Garrard, on his 1911 expedition to retrieve penguin eggs in the Antarctic.

'Those who need to ask, will never understand the answer, while others who feel the answer will never need to ask.'
Wally Herbert, the first man to reach the North Pole unsupported, in answer to the question 'Why?'

THE COLDEST PLACES IN THE WORLD

The Arctic and Antarctic lands are places where world records are broken. Here you will find the most extreme conditions: the coldest, the windiest, the driest – not forgetting some of the *most dangerous* conditions ever experienced by humans.

Why are they called the polar lands?

Because they are found at the very ends – or poles – of the earth. The earth spins on an imaginary axis at the top end of which is the North Pole and at the bottom end the South Pole (see opposite).

What is the North Pole?

The most northern point on the earth's axis, which sits in the middle of the Arctic Circle. Its full name is the Geographic North Pole.

What is the South Pole?

The most southern point on the earth's axis, which sits in the middle of the Antarctic Circle. Its full name is the Geographic South Pole.

Why are the polar lands so cold?

Because they don't get enough sun to warm them up.

Are the Arctic and Antarctic lands similar?

No. The term 'poles apart' is very appropriate when talking about the polar lands because they are different in many ways.

THE POLAR LANDS

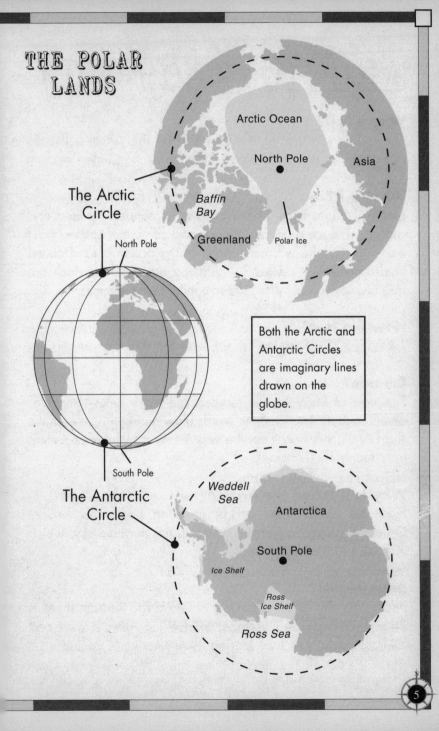

Arctic Ocean

North Pole

Asia

The Arctic Circle

Baffin Bay

Greenland

Polar Ice

North Pole

South Pole

The Antarctic Circle

Both the Arctic and Antarctic Circles are imaginary lines drawn on the globe.

Weddell Sea

Antarctica

South Pole

Ice Shelf

Ross Ice Shelf

Ross Sea

ARCTIC KNOW-HOW

Where is it?
The region surrounding the North Pole. The Arctic is usually thought of as being the area inside the Arctic Circle.

What is it?
Much of it is a huge frozen ocean (surrounded by land and islands). The ice is always moving and can crack open without warning. On the warmer fringes of the ocean is land called tundra (meaning 'treeless') – swampy grass plains which are free of snow and ice for a few months in the summer.

How big is it?
14,056,000 square km, about twice the size of Australia.

Climate?
For most of the year, the temperature stays below freezing, often reaching –40°C. Bitter winds blow during this time. In the short Arctic summer, it can be very sunny and the temperature may reach 10°C.

Why is it called the Arctic?
From the Greek word *arktos*, meaning bear. The Ancient Greeks observed a group of stars in the northern sky, which they said looked like a bear.

Days/nights?
Because of the Arctic's position in relation to the sun, there is 24-hour darkness in December (during the Arctic winter) and 24-hour daylight in June (during its summer).

Countries/nearest countries?
(Some are in the Arctic Circle.)
Canada, Greenland, Iceland, Norway, Sweden, Finland, Russia, USA (Alaska).

Animals?
Yes, these include polar bears, whales, walruses and seals as well as arctic wolves, foxes, hares, herds of reindeer and musk oxen on the land around the edges of the ocean. There are also many birds and fish.

Plants?
Yes, grass, flowers and moss on the land during the short Arctic summer.

People?
Yes, the Inuit people in northern Canada and other native peoples in Greenland, northern Scandinavia and northern Russia. These people have lived in these areas for thousands of years. Their ancestors probably walked across the frozen ice to get here.

The Arctic

Extent of ice in winter

Russian Federation

Alaska

Bering Strait

North America

Extent of ice in summer

Severnaya Zemlya

Asia

North Pole

Franz Josef Land

Hudson Bay Strait

Baffin Bay

Baffin Island

Novaya Zemlya

Davis Strait

Greenland

Spitzbergen

Barents Sea

Iceland

Europe

Scandinavia

Atlantic Ocean

ANTARCTIC KNOW-HOW

Where is it?
The region surrounding the South Pole. Most of the continent of Antarctica is contained within the Antarctic Circle.

What is it?
A huge land mass, an ice-covered continent. In fact the western part is really made up of islands, but they are joined together by the ice on top of them. It is very mountainous in places – 4,897 metres high at one point.

How big is it?
13,900,000 square km, or about the same size as the USA and Mexico combined.

Climate?
The coldest place in the world (has reached –89.6°C) and also extremely dry, with very little rainfall. Hurricane-force winds and blizzards make it extremely unpleasant for humans.

Why is it called the Antarctic?
From the Greek word *antarktos*, meaning 'opposite the bear'.

Days/nights?
There is 24-hour darkness in June (during the long Antarctic winter) and 24-hour daylight in December (during its short summer). This is the opposite of the Arctic.

Nearest countries? (None is inside the Antarctic Circle.)
Chile, Australia, New Zealand, South Africa.

Animals?
Yes, penguins and other birds. In the seas around the continent there are whales, seals, dolphins, porpoises, fish and other smaller sea creatures, like plankton.

Plants?
Yes, mosses and lichens on bare areas of rock that are not covered by snow or ice.

People?
Nowadays, yes: bases and field camps of scientists from all over the world, including geologists, biologists, physicists (looking at the atmosphere and other things) and glaciologists (studying ice). Nobody lived in Antarctica before the twentieth century.

The Antarctic

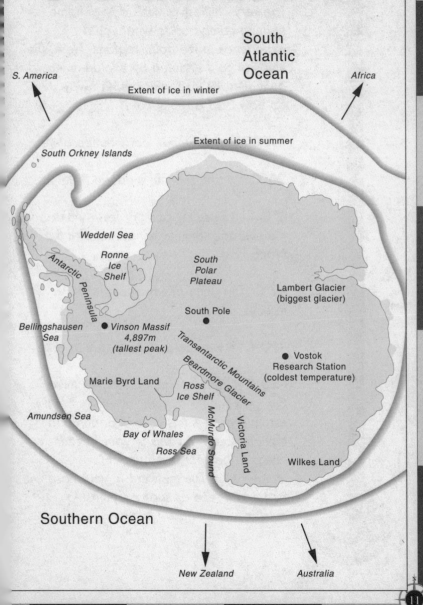

South
Atlantic
Ocean

S. America

Africa

Extent of ice in winter

Extent of ice in summer

South Orkney Islands

Weddell Sea

Ronne
Ice
Shelf

South
Polar
Plateau

Lambert Glacier
(biggest glacier)

Antarctic Peninsula

South Pole

Bellingshausen
Sea

Vinson Massif
4,897m
(tallest peak)

Transantarctic Mountains

Vostok
Research Station
(coldest temperature)

Marie Byrd Land

Beardmore Glacier

Ross
Ice Shelf

Amundsen Sea

Victoria Land

Bay of Whales

McMurdo Sound

Ross Sea

Wilkes Land

Southern Ocean

New Zealand

Australia

FEELING THE COLD

The very chilliest winter's day at home is nothing compared to what you'd experience in the polar regions. Here, the kinds of cold endured by explorers would quite literally take your breath away. So how cold is really cold?

37°C Normal human body temperature.

25°C A warm summer's day in Britain.

0°C The freezing point of fresh water and the average summer temperature at the North Pole.

–2°C The point at which sea water freezes.

–10°C A very cold winter's day in Britain.

–20°C It can drop to this temperature in Europe's Alpine regions in winter, but it rarely ever gets this cold in Britain and lowland Europe. Food in your freezer needs to be kept at around this temperature. The moisture in your nose will begin to freeze as soon as you step outside.

−30 to **−35°C** An average winter temperature for the Arctic. An unpleasant temperature for humans, even when wearing special protective clothing. Exposed skin will begin to freeze if a person is not moving around much.

−40 to **−50°C** A cold winter's day on coastal Antarctica (which is not as cold as the central and higher parts). Walking outside becomes dangerous. Exposed flesh will freeze very quickly, first turning white, then blistering. If left untreated, the flesh could eventually turn black and die from gangrene (see page 56).

−60°C About the average winter temperature at the South Pole. Most people would find it unbearable to be outside.

−70°C The lowest temperature recorded in the Arctic, at Nord Station, Greenland.

−89.6°C The lowest temperature ever recorded in the world, taken at the Vostok Research Station in Antarctica in 1983. If you threw boiling water into the air it would freeze immediately.

These temperatures don't take the effect of the wind into account. The strength and speed of the wind, the wind-chill factor, has a huge effect on temperature and its impact on the human body. (See page 95.)

SOMETHING ALL EXPLORERS HAVE TO KNOW

Any adventurer to an unknown land needs to know exactly where they are and where they're going. To find out, lines called **latitude** and **longitude** are used. These are imaginary lines that cut up the world. Exact measurements of latitude and longitude are made in degrees (written °) and smaller measurements called minutes (written '), e.g. the position of London is 51°30'N, 00°05'W. One degree is equivalent to about 111 km and one minute is about 1.85 km.

Explorers used these lines to measure how far they had gone compared to others before them.

*Lines of **latitude** are measured from the equator, an imaginary horizontal line that runs across the middle of the earth. They give distances in degrees north and south of the equator. 1°N (north) is just above the equator, 1°S (south) is just below it.*

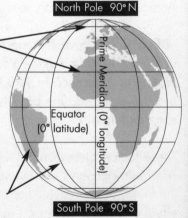

*Lines of **longitude** are measured from the prime meridian, an imaginary vertical line running across the middle of the earth. They give distances in degrees east or west of the prime meridian. The Poles are found where lines of longitude meet at the top and bottom of the globe.*

SEARCHING FOR THE ENDS OF THE EARTH

Until about 500 years ago most people believed the world was flat, and assumed that an adventurous traveller would simply fall off the edge of the earth into a dark nothingness!

Many also thought that if you ventured too far from home you would come across terrible horrors. Frightening stories were told of things that would put all but the bravest sailors off exploring too far. They described not only falling off the end of the world, but also:

• Northern seas with fogs so thick they could suffocate you.

• Terrifying giant sea monsters that blew out water and could capsize a small ship (these were probably whales!). 'Here be dragons' was said to be written on early maps as a warning for sailors.

• Other weird creatures with long teeth (probably walruses!).

However, in the fifteenth century things began to change. Brave sailors from various European countries began to set out on long sea voyages to unknown places, looking for riches and rewards.

Would you be brave enough to face unknown horrors, just as the early explorers did?

Often these journeys were to search for new trade routes. The sailors and their sponsors hoped to get lucky and very rich from their discoveries. The 'Age of Exploration' had begun.

Many of these explorers were able to use an ancient Greek map which had only been discovered in 1478. This map showed the Greek idea of a *round* world, with the top end named *artktos* and the bottom *antarktos* (see pages 6 and 9).

Some of the Ancient Greeks had got the shape of the world right, approximately 1,300 years earlier! And now that so many voyages of discovery were being made, adventurers could add to this knowledge and make new, more accurate maps. The idea that the world was flat was eventually forgotten.

One of the directions in which fifteenth- and sixteenth-century explorers set out was northwards, up and away from their own European countries.

Very, very early travellers in very, very northern seas

From old writings it seems that the first-ever polar explorer lived in the fourth century BC (Before Christ). He was a brave Phoenician sailor, called Pytheas, from Massilia in the south of France (now called Marseilles) and he probably sailed as far north as Iceland.

Ancient texts tell us that 1,000 years later Irish monks travelled to these same northern waters in little leather-covered boats called coracles. They described mermaids, talking birds and even a whale that let them cook a pot of stew on its back!

About 300 years or so after this (AD 800–1100) Vikings from Norway and Denmark reached Iceland, Greenland and what is now called Newfoundland.

Very, very early travellers in very, very southern seas

The Polynesian people, on the Pacific islands, tell the story of an ancient chief called Ui-te-Rangiora who travelled in about AD 650 until he reached a frozen sea.

EARLY DISCOVERIES AND DISAPPEARANCES

LET'S GO BY BOAT TO CHINA!

The early explorers into the Arctic Circle were not actually looking for the Arctic. They were searching for a new route to India and China. For hundreds of years, spices and exotic goods, like silk, had come to Europe overland from Asia, over high mountains and across hot deserts in long camel trains. These Silk Route goods were sold for vast amounts of money when they reached the markets of Europe.

The Portuguese and Spanish had already found sea routes to the east via the bottom of South Africa and South America. English, French and Dutch explorers wanted to see if there were any shorter routes to China across the top of the world. They were very brave because no Europeans of this time knew what really existed up there!

They thought that there could be two possible routes north from Europe:

• 'The North-east Passage' ➡️
Was there maybe a sea route to China to the east, along the top of Scandinavia and then over the top of Russia?

• 'The North-west Passage' ⬅️
Could there be a route going west over the top of North America?

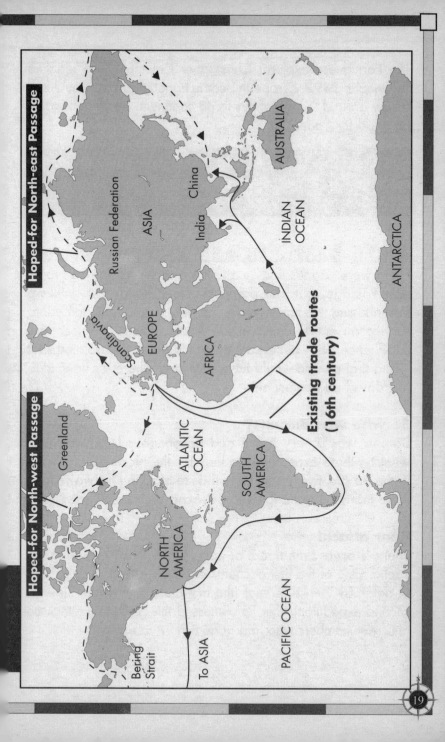

Hoped-for North-west Passage

Hoped-for North-east Passage

Greenland

Russian Federation

Scandinavia

ASIA

EUROPE

China

India

AFRICA

ATLANTIC
OCEAN

AUSTRALIA

INDIAN
OCEAN

ANTARCTICA

**Existing trade routes
(16th century)**

NORTH
AMERICA

Bering
Strait

To ASIA

SOUTH
AMERICA

PACIFIC OCEAN

The Portuguese explorer Christopher Columbus had reached America in 1492. European people hoped that they would find a way around the top of this large continent, because it would be good for trade.

The first brave Europeans to try to find these uncharted 'passages' were quite literally sailing into the unknown. What adventures were lying ahead for them?

NORTH-EAST PASSAGE NIGHTMARE

There were various early expeditions to search for the North-east Passage, but one particular story stands out. William Barents and his crew were the first Europeans forced to survive an entire winter in the Arctic. It was a horrendous experience. They believed they would die in this isolated spot – and that no one would have any idea where, or how, their last days had been spent.

So who was Barents?

Barents was a very brave and adventurous Dutchman who went on three expeditions to look for the North-east Passage in the 1590s. Every time he found ice blocking his way. There were many other dangers to be faced such as polar bears.

Bear attack!

There is always the threat of polar bears when exploring the Arctic. One of the first accounts of a bear attack is described in detail by Gerrit de Veer (the first mate on William Barents' second expedition) after he witnessed this gruesome attack on his crew members who had gone ashore to explore:

A great leane white bear came sodainly stealing out, and caught one of them fast by the necke, who not knowing what it was that tooke him by the necke, cried out and said, 'Who is that pulles me so by the necke?' Wherewith the other, that lay not farre from him, lifted up his head to see who it was, and perceiving it to be a monsterous beare, cryed and sayd, 'Oh mate it is a beare!' and therewith presently rose up and ran away.

The bear began to eat its victim as the terrified sailors watched. Twenty men ran towards the creature with muskets and pikes to try to rescue the body, but the fierce animal seized another of the men and ate him alive too. Eventually one of the crew managed to shoot the bear between the eyes. Gerrit de Veer describes the bear rearing up with the body still in its mouth before it finally staggered and fell to the ground with a last roar.

Surviving the Arctic winter

But despite his encounters with ice and fierce polar bears, Barents set off on a third expedition in 1596–7. This time the ship got completely stuck north of Russia, off the northern coast of Novaya Zemlya (which means the New Land). The ship became crushed as if in a vice, among the ice-floes and icebergs and it was impossible to rescue her. Barents and the crew of sixteen had to spend the entire winter in a bay, building themselves a house from driftwood they found on a beach. The house was built in Dutch style with a high roof made from a sail, a funnel-like chimney made from an old beer barrel, and tall doors. It didn't do a good job of keeping the men warm, particularly as the walls were only made of 4-cm planks of wood. A fire blazed in the middle of the house but the men found that their feet would get warm while their backsides were still freezing! It was so cold that everything froze: the men's muskets, their clothes and all their food and drink.

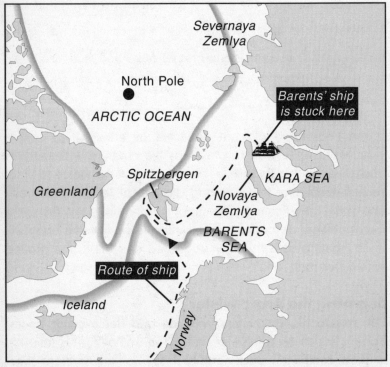

But there were other problems of survival beyond the need for warmth and shelter ...

Hunting for food

Once their supplies had run out, the men had to hunt to get food, by setting traps for arctic foxes or by trying to shoot one of the many polar bears around, always a dangerous task. The skin of one of the polar bears they caught was 3.5 metres in length! The men used the bears' skins for clothes and their fat for lamp fuel during the dark, dark winter months.

One night they made a stew from two bears' livers. Over the next few days many of the men became so ill that they thought they were dying. We now know that they were probably badly poisoned. A bear's liver contains an enormous amount of vitamin A and it was only in the 1920s that it was discovered that it is possible to die from consuming too much of this vitamin (see page 98 for a horrible story about such a poisoning). The native peoples of the Arctic will always leave a bear's liver, and even their dogs seldom touch it.

Spring thaw

Despite the bears, the illnesses and the freezing conditions, Barents and most of his men managed to survive the winter. After ten months, spring came and they started to prepare two small open boats for the seas. In June they set off, hoping beyond hope that they would reach Holland and home. And most of them did. Barents himself died (from either exhaustion or scurvy) on the journey but twelve of his original crew of sixteen survived.

Excitement in Europe

This was the first time that any Europeans had ever survived a winter so far north (latitude 76°N). A thrilling account of Barents' three expeditions was published, which described the adventures of the unfortunate 'castaways'. It had one of the longest titles of any book (three whole paragraphs) which enticed the public with accounts of icy places:

'...Where never any man had been before: with the Cruel Bears and other Monsters of the Sea.'

The book became a best-seller!

In 1871 the remains of Barents' driftwood house were found by the captain of a Norwegian seal-hunting boat. The roof had fallen in and it had obviously been explored on numerous occasions by polar bears. Many of the men's belongings were still preserved in the ice. This find was also evidence that the men's account of their horrendous winter was a true story.

EXTREME FACTS
POLAR BEARS

Arctic explorers must be constantly on the look-out for polar bears. They are extremely aggressive and powerful animals. If they are hungry, they will attack any creature, including humans. Polar bears are bigger than any other type of bear, in fact a fully grown bear is nearly twice as tall as a human being, and perhaps ten times heavier! One swipe of a paw can kill a person.

Helen Thayer, who made a solo journey to the Magnetic North Pole in 1988, tells of several terrifying encounters with polar bears. In one of them a fully grown male suddenly appeared from behind a hummock of ice, just 6 metres away. He rose up on his hind legs and then charged at her. She shot at the bear (and missed) but luckily her faithful husky dog, Charlie, came to the rescue. Sinking his teeth into one of the bear's legs, he hung on for dear life until the bear had had enough and finally ran off, leaving one very shaken explorer!

This is what explorers are advised to do if they come across an aggressive polar bear:

1) Stay calm!
2) Don't run.
3) Keep eye contact with the bear.
4) Never move backwards (only sideways or forwards).
5) If possible, stand beside a large object so it makes you look bigger (e.g. a tent)
6) Don't shoot unless you absolutely have to, and if you do, make sure you kill the bear. If you only wound the bear you will make it even more dangerous.
7) And most important of all ... try not to show you are frightened!

> **Samoyeds**
> Barents met some locals called the Samoyeds on his
> voyages to look for the North-east Passage. These nomadic
> people lived on the very north coast of Russia – and their
> descendants still live there today. The Samoyeds hunted
> reindeer with bows and arrows.

So does the North-east Passage actually exist?

Yes! However, it is usually blocked by ice (as Barents found). It wasn't sailed along until the 1870s – by a Swedish ship, the *Vega*, which spent nine months stuck in ice just off the coast of Siberia. Nowadays icebreakers (big, strong ships which are specially designed to cut a way through the ice) make it possible for the journey to be made.

NORTH-WEST PASSAGE NIGHTMARE

Many early expeditions tried to sail north and then west through the large islands along the top of North America in the search for trade routes. Explorers Verrazano, Cartier and Frobisher all made great achievements in their journeys (see Timeline, page 135). In the mid 1570s, an Englishman called Davis carefully recorded much of the sea and land between Greenland and Canada (Davis Strait is named after him). However, late summer ice stopped him from going further north. This *was* the way to the entrance to the North-west Passage, but it was to be another twenty years before a European tried this route out.

HUDSON'S HORRENDOUS HAPPENINGS

Henry Hudson was an English adventurer who explored the area around the Hudson River in 1609 (where New York now stands), so giving it his name.

In 1610 he was financed by English merchants to travel north again on his ship, *Discovery*. The aim of the expedition was to explore the strait (now known as Hudson Strait) at the bottom of Baffin Island, which previous sailors had discovered and mapped. The *Discovery* had a crew of twenty and two boys, one of whom was Hudson's son Jack, who was only sixteen.

Hudson sailed along the strait for 1,120 km and eventually found what he thought was open sea. He turned south with great excitement and carried on, thinking that he was entering the Pacific Ocean and that he had found the North-west Passage! Unfortunately for him the *Discovery* had actually ended up in the

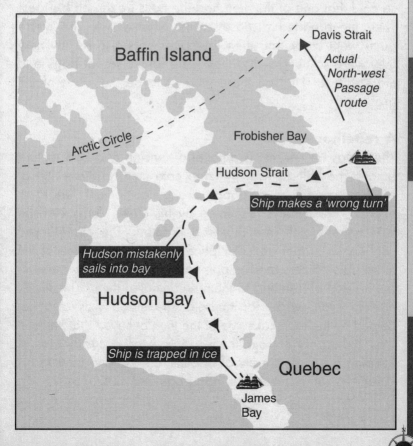

world's largest bay (Hudson Bay, in what is now Canada). It was a dead end – an enormous trap. As the land began to close in on them, Hudson and his crew realized their mistake. But it was too late and there was no time to turn north and sail home before winter set in.

The *Discovery* got stuck in the ice in James Bay. Although this bay is below the Arctic Circle it is still very cold in winter and the crew did not have suitable clothing or enough food. They began to suffer from starvation (as food had to be rationed) as well as the effects of the freezing climate. It was so cold that one of the men had the nails frozen off his toes! Then the dreaded disease, scurvy, broke out. The men's gums went black and their jawbones began to rot. By now they were so hungry that they were forced to eat frogs and moss. But for Hudson these weren't to be the worst of the problems.

A rebellious crew

There was an enormous amount of tension and bad feeling among the half-starved, freezing cold men. In these sort of extreme conditions a good, strong, competent leader is needed, one who is respected by his crew. Henry Hudson was unfortunately not that sort of man. The men lacked confidence in him and discipline broke down. Some of the more able officers tried to point out the problems to Hudson, but instead of listening to them he demoted them! This made matters even worse for himself. The mood was also not helped by the fact that some of the men believed that Hudson was hiding food from them. They later accused him of keeping a private supply of biscuits, cheese and beer in his cabin – a rather nicer diet than frogs and moss!

So what happened to Hudson and his team of not so merry men?

After seven long dreadful months, eventually summer came and the ice thawed enough to release the ship. 'Great,' thought the crew. 'At last we are going home!' But Hudson had very different ideas. He announced that they were all going to continue the search for the North-west Passage by sailing north out of James Bay and then west!

By now the crew of the *Discovery* had had enough of Hudson. After all their suffering, they weren't going home! They turned against him in a mutiny, even though they knew this was a crime they could be hanged for when they got back to Europe. But they didn't care. They weren't going through another winter like the one they had just spent.

Alone at sea

In their anger, the mutineers forced Hudson, his son, Jack, and a few loyal and sick sailors into a small boat that they set adrift in the open sea – giving them just a small bag of meat to survive on. Hudson and the others knew they were facing almost certain death. We can only try to imagine how they must have felt watching the *Discovery*, their only hope of survival, sail away from them.

The small boat and its crew were never seen again.

Only nine of the thirteen mutineers eventually got back to the British Isles on the *Discovery*. Immediately after getting rid of Hudson, they fought over the remaining food, which didn't last very long. After many more weeks at sea, they all became very weak and ill. Several of the ringleaders died in a fight with some local people when they went ashore to hunt for food on the journey home. The remaining crew were forced to live on seaweed fried in candle grease. They were a sorry sight when they finally reached Ireland, lying on the deck, sick with scurvy and starvation.

This painting shows Hudson and his son as they are left, stranded, to die in the open sea.

EXTREME FACTS
SCURVY – THE SAILORS' DISEASE

This was a big, big problem for explorers and sailors in early times. No one knew what caused scurvy, but as it often happened to people on very long sea journeys, some thought it to be caused by the lack of mental and physical exercise. We now know that scurvy is caused by a lack of vitamin C, which you find in fresh food, especially fruit and vegetables. This is exactly the kind of food people didn't get on early expeditions.

The signs of scurvy are:
- bleeding, swollen, blackened and spongy gums, so you can't eat because your mouth is too sore
- teeth getting loose and falling out
- arms and legs getting very stiff and painful, eventually becoming discoloured and swollen
- sores coming out on the skin

If left untreated the symptoms just get worse and worse until the person dies. In 1619, a Danish expedition made a voyage into Hudson Bay, where they were forced to spend the winter. The leader, Jens Munk, had to watch as scurvy killed off nearly all his men 'with great pains in the loins, as if a thousand knives were thrust through them.' There were only three survivors.

However, in the Arctic, the Inuit people didn't get scurvy. Why? Well, it was because they ate raw meat which contains vitamin C. (Barents' men probably stopped themselves getting scurvy without realizing it by eating half-raw arctic foxes).

Two whole centuries were to pass before anyone else recorded sailing further north.

There was not much time to go exploring in the short Arctic summers, and in some years, as Davis had found, the pack-ice thawed less than in others. No one wanted to spend the winter stuck in the ice. They didn't have the clothes or food for it.

Clothes and equipment

The early European explorers wore woollen shirts, felt jackets and leather boots. These were just the ordinary clothes worn for a European winter. They had not been specially adapted for the extreme conditions the men were experiencing.

- European clothes were twice as heavy as the fur clothing the native Arctic people wore, but not nearly as warm.

- One of the really big problems was that when the clothes got damp they could no longer keep the heat in and then just froze. The furs the native people of the Arctic wore had been designed by nature to repel water.

Neither did the early European explorers have any special equipment for these extreme conditions. For example, their tents were just the normal ones they would use in Europe.

- They did not keep the explorers warm in the icy cold. The tents were made of heavy canvas, which lost any insulating properties when it got damp, and froze.

- The tents were also difficult to carry around and took ages to put up. In contrast the native people's igloos took only one hour to build and were also much, much warmer. Igloos are built from blocks of ice and the cracks between these are filled in with snow.

MORE ARCTIC ADVENTURES

When England finished fighting wars against France and Napoleon in 1815, it had a very big navy and very little for the sailors to do. It was decided to use the Royal Navy to go on expeditions to find out more about the Arctic and the Antarctic, and especially to see if there was a North-west Passage in the Arctic.

Parliament decided to offer cash prizes to those searching for the North-west Passage – £5,000 for the first person to reach 110°W, £10,000 for 130°W, £15,000 for 150°W and £20,000 for reaching the Pacific. These were enormous sums of money in those days! Many sailors set off to try to find the passage. Parry, Ross and Franklin are among the names that feature (see Timeline, page 135).

A MYSTERIOUS DISAPPEARANCE

Sir John Franklin was a Scotsman who, as a member of the Royal Navy, had been exploring in the waters of the Arctic Circle since 1819. In 1845 he set off from Britain with a very large, and confident, British naval expedition of 137 men and two ships, HMS *Erebus* and HMS *Terror*. They had provisions for three years and were very hopeful of finally proving that there *was* a North-west Passage.

This journey was hailed as the greatest Arctic expedition of all time. There was great excitement in Britain as the men set off, but three years later that excitement had died down. There had been no news at all of the expedition during this time and people were starting to get very worried. What had happened? Where were the men? Were any of them still alive?

The British Admiralty offered a reward of £20,000 for news of Franklin and his men.

Over the following years, forty expeditions set off to look for them. What they found made the case of the missing men even more mysterious.

The Franklin 'Finds'
1850: Graves
The graves of three bodies (crew members) were discovered on the shore of Beechey Island. Near by were the remains of a store house, a garden and several look-out platforms – along with a pile of 700 empty tin cans.

Why had they died? And where were the other men – and their two ships?

1854: Sighting
The first bit of positive news surfaced. Some Inuit (see page 52) told a Scottish explorer that, several years before, they had seen a large group of white men pulling a sledge along the Great Fish River. The Inuits also had some silver spoons, buttons and even a medal – all apparently from the Franklin expedition. This backed up their story.

1857: Skeletons
Franklin's wife, Lady Jane, hired an experienced Arctic explorer from Ireland, Captain McClintock, to search for her husband. In the spring of 1859 he found a human skeleton dressed in a steward's uniform. In a cairn (a mound of stones) near by, he found a canister containing a piece of paper with two messages from Franklin and his men.

The first message was dated May 1847 and said that all was well. The men had spent their first winter on Beechey Island and the second on King William Island.

However, a second, more worrying, message had been written around the edge of the paper two years later. It was signed by Franklin's deputies, Crozier and James. They said

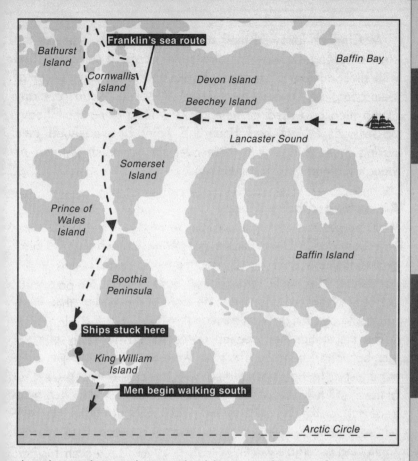

that the *Erebus* and *Terror* had been stuck in ice for nineteen months. Franklin and twenty-three other men had died. The others had decided to leave the ships and try to walk south to the Great Fish River.

Stupid, stupid, stupid ...

This seemed an incredibly stupid idea because, if help had arrived, it would have come from the waters to the north. It was a very, very long walk over the bare tundra to Hudson Bay. What were the men thinking of?

McClintock followed their route. He found skeletons of the crew all along the way. He also came across a sledge loaded with silver cutlery, cigar cases, books and other objects – all of them completely useless for survival. It looked as though many of the men had died in their tracks while pulling their heavy possessions. What had been the point of weakened men pulling these things with them over the snow? It seemed as though the men had lost their senses.

An extraordinary theory

Well, maybe the men *had* lost their senses. In 1984 a professor from Canada, Dr Owen Beattie, got permission to dig up the three graves first found in 1850. The men had been buried in the permafrost (the Arctic ground that never thaws) so they were perfectly preserved. However, the sight of the bodies was still a gruesome one for Dr Beattie's team.

The first coffin they opened up contained the body of crew member John Torrington. The team were amazed to see him lying there just as he had been buried, with half-closed eyes gazing up at them, still fully dressed in his Victorian clothes. He looked quite peaceful, unlike the second man they dug up, John Hartnell, whose snarling expression gave them all a shock. Had he died some kind of terrible death?

The coffin of William Braine was the final one to be opened. Dr Beattie performed various tests on the bodies, which gave some very interesting results. They showed that each body had strong traces of lead in the hair. Could this have had something to do with their deaths? Beattie thought so.

But how? Well, Franklin's expedition was using one of the newest technologies of the time – tinned food. Some of the tins were still around and when Beattie examined them he saw that they had been closed with lead solder. This had leaked into the food inside.

When the body of Able-bodied Seaman, John Hartnell, was excavated, the whole team was shocked at the sight of the corpse.

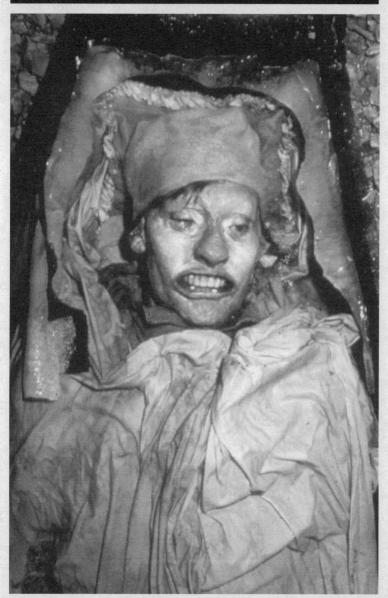

The body of Royal Marine Private William Braine was the third and final one to be excavated.

Lead is an extremely dangerous substance if it is absorbed by the human body. It damages organs and affects the mind. A person can become mad and even die from lead poisoning. Dr Beattie's tests showed that Franklin and his men were slowly poisoned by the lead in the food they were eating, which made them more likely to get other diseases and unable to make proper decisions. It seems tragic that the men had gone all this way, only to have been finally killed off by tins of food!

Bodies from the expedition's astonishing march continue to be found, some as recently as 1994. There has never been any trace of the two ships.

But Franklin's expedition did achieve something ...

All the expeditions sent to look for Franklin helped to increase geographical knowledge of the area, and by the end of the 1850s much of the Arctic coastline had been mapped.

So does the North-west Passage exist?

Yes, it does.

When was it found?

The first full crossing (though not sailing) was made in the 1850s by Robert McClure. While searching for the Franklin expedition, he had tried to sail through the North-west Passage from the Pacific side, through the Bering Strait. McClure and his men ended up being rescued and walking out on the Atlantic side after their ship got stuck in ice.

The first boat to sail from one end to the other was the *Gjøa*, on a 1903–6 expedition. Its leader was a young Norwegian called Amundsen, a man who was later to become extremely famous in polar exploration (see page 79).

GOING SOUTH – ICE, ICE AND MORE ICE

At the beginning of the seventeenth century the very bottom part of the world was marked on maps as one enormous continent called 'Terra Australis Incognita', the 'Unknown Southern Land'. But no one really knew what was there.

Then, in the 1640s, a Dutch sailor called Abel Tasman sailed around Australia and brought news of this continent back to Europe, but it was to be another 100 years before Captain James Cook charted the east coast and claimed it for Britain. 'So was that it?' European explorers wondered. 'Was Australia *the* great southern continent? Or is there something else further south?'

In 1772 Captain Cook set out again to see if there was any large area of land south of Australia. He crossed into the Antarctic Circle (the first person recorded to have done so) but only found ice, ice and more ice. He was very unlucky and never managed to see any of the continent of Antarctica itself, despite the fact that he actually sailed right round it. He came to the conclusion that there was no land south of Australia that people could live on.

Cook's experiences in these seas put off other potential explorers and there were fewer expeditions to the bottom of the world than to the top, but fifty years later, a Russian expedition reported seeing land here.

Naming new discoveries

Then, in 1823 James Weddell, a Scots sealing captain, reached as far as 74°15'S to a stretch of water now known as the Weddell Sea. Weddell was very lucky to have got this far because this sea is usually full of dangerous icebergs. He also found a new type of seal which is now named after him – the Weddell Seal. This seal lives further south than any other seal.

Another explorer of this time whose name also lives on in the Antarctic is Scotsman James Clark Ross. Ross set sail in 1839 in *Erebus* and *Terror* (the very same ships Franklin would later use on his ill-fated expedition in 1845 – see page 34), and managed to make a way through the pack-ice to an enormous ice shelf, where cliffs towered 60 metres above the small ships. Now called after him, the Ross Ice Shelf stretches into the continent, forming an enormous area of ice the size of France. He then discovered Ross Island, where he named the two volcanoes Mount Erebus and Mount Terror. The bay was called McMurdo Sound after the *Terror*'s first lieutenant.

The Ross Sea was also named after this explorer. It is the best approach route to the Antarctic continent because the ice here loosens and melts during most summers.

EXTREME FACTS
ICY WATERS

Ships sailing to the Arctic or Antarctic were faced with the danger of crashing into icebergs and other large pieces of ice as well as the constant threat of getting stuck in the ice. Here are some of the different kinds of ice formation the explorers would have encountered:

Ice shelf
An ice shelf is an enormous area of ice which is permanently attached to the land, often in a large bay. From the sea an ice shelf can look like a series of large white cliffs running along the shoreline.

Glaciers
A glacier is a great mass of ice and snow that moves slowly under its own weight. The largest glacier in the world is the Lambert Glacier in Antarctica, which is 400 km long and over 40 km wide. It then flows on to an

ice shelf and reaches the sea 300 km later, where it is 200 km wide. In the mountains it moves at about 230 metres per year.

Icebergs

Icebergs are large chunks of floating ice that have broken off a glacier or ice shelf. They can be any size from that of a small house to the area of a large town. The most famous ship ever to hit an iceberg was the *Titanic* in 1912, when she was sailing between Southampton, England, and New York, USA – 1,513 lives were lost.

Antarctic icebergs are even bigger than Arctic ones. Icebergs can last for up to six years and they gradually melt as they drift into warmer regions.

Ice-floes

Ice-floes are large flat pieces of floating ice, any size from a metre to several metres.

Pack-ice

Pack-ice is when the sea has large ice-floes floating in it. These move around with the winds and currents. In storms and in rough seas the ice-floes crash together and get pushed up on top of each other; some even get stuck upright! A ship can make a way through the channels of water between the pack-ice but the crew must watch out as winter approaches because the ice-floes can close in and trap, or, sometimes, even crush the vessel. This has happened to many explorers whose ships have become stuck in the ice for months or even years.

TO THE NORTH POLE — OR NOT?

Is it possible to reach the North Pole?
What will we find there?

These were the questions that European explorers were asking themselves during the time of Arctic exploration in the nineteenth century. Some people suggested that the frozen sea that explorers had found so far was just an outer ring. Perhaps there was an enormous unfrozen sea beyond all the ice, where the North Pole lay?

Whatever there was, it was a mystery that people wanted to solve.

NANSEN GOES WITH THE FLOW

An Arctic explorer from Norway called Fridtjof Nansen got very excited in 1884 when he heard that some Inuit had found wreckage of an American ship called the *Jeanette*. This ship had disappeared three years earlier in the Bering Strait. But it had been found on the south-west coast of Greenland, a mammoth 2,900 nautical miles from where it had last been heard of. Nansen thought that the *Jeanette* must have been carried along by an ocean drift across the Arctic. He decided to study this further and ended up planning a most unusual expedition.

Most explorers do everything they can *not* to get stuck in the ice. Nansen did the opposite. He decided to take a ship and *deliberately* get stuck, then stay on board to see where he and the ship ended up! He was sure that the ocean drift would take him directly to the North Pole. Therefore he arranged to have a special ship built that would not be crushed when the pressure of the ice closed in on it (as had happened to so many others before).

A lot of people thought he was mad, but in his homeland they were so enthusiastic that Nansen was given an enormous sum of money to enable him to build his ship, the *Fram* (meaning *Forward*).

The *Fram* was the first ship ever to be built specially to enter a polar region. It was a very wide ship – nearly a third as wide as it was long (36 metres long by 10 metres wide) – and had a rounded hull (bottom). Nansen believed that this would allow the ship to be lifted up rather than crushed as the ice pressed in on her.

Using the knowledge of the native peoples

Nansen was a very experienced Arctic explorer. He had led a team of six men across Greenland on skis from east to west, the first time that anyone had done this. On this trip Nansen had used his knowledge of the survival skills used by native Arctic people to travel, eat and keep warm.

The native peoples of the Arctic made their clothes out of skin and fur. These were the best possible materials they could have used for the very cold climate they lived and worked in. They wore two layers of clothes, which trapped air in between them – this is one of the best forms of insulation. If you want to keep warm, wear several layers of clothes rather than one heavy item!

This complete outfit only weighed about 5 kg, half as much as early European-style clothes. Remember, you need to conserve energy to help you survive in these very cold places, so the lighter your clothes are the better – as long as they keep you toasty warm of course! Until the Europeans really began to study what the native peoples were wearing, they were using up a huge amount of unnecessary energy just to keep warm.

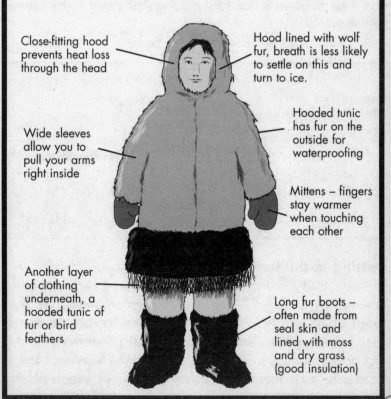

Close-fitting hood prevents heat loss through the head

Hood lined with wolf fur, breath is less likely to settle on this and turn to ice.

Hooded tunic has fur on the outside for waterproofing

Wide sleeves allow you to pull your arms right inside

Mittens – fingers stay warmer when touching each other

Another layer of clothing underneath, a hooded tunic of fur or bird feathers

Long fur boots – often made from seal skin and lined with moss and dry grass (good insulation)

Polar expedition food

Nansen and other Arctic explorers began to take provisions on their expeditions that were based on the food of the native Arctic peoples. One of these items was called pemmican. This was dried beef, pounded into a powder and mixed with melted beef fat. Polar explorers moulded it into blocks, enough to last one man for a day. These blocks were then melted with hot water (heated-up snow) at night to turn them into 'hoosh', a kind of thick soup. Often biscuits and anything else available would be added to this.

The Arctic explorers also took seal meat with them to prevent scurvy. They had to plan and pack all the food for themselves and their dogs very carefully as *everything* had to be carried with them.

A typical day's menu would have been:

Breakfast:
Hoosh

***

Lunch:
Snack of dried fish (to be eaten on the move)

***

Dinner:
Speciality of the day – another (very large) serving of hoosh!

Drifting in the ice

In June 1893 the *Fram* set off north from Norway. Including Nansen, there were 12 men and 30 dogs on board. The *Fram* sailed along the North-east Passage route across the top of Scandinavia and Siberia. Towards the end of September the ship was above the mouth of the River Lena. It was here that Nansen wanted the ice to trap the *Fram* as winter drew in. Would the ship live up to Nansen's expectations?

The ice closed in and … the *Fram* was lifted up, not crushed! There was great excitement on board. Nansen had been proved right about his ship's design. But was he right about the Atlantic Ocean Drift?

Going the wrong way

At first it all seemed a great mistake. For six weeks the ice-stuck *Fram* drifted in exactly the opposite direction to the one expected. However, in December the direction of the drift changed and the ship returned to its original position. Then, finally, it began to move towards the Pole, as Nansen had hoped.

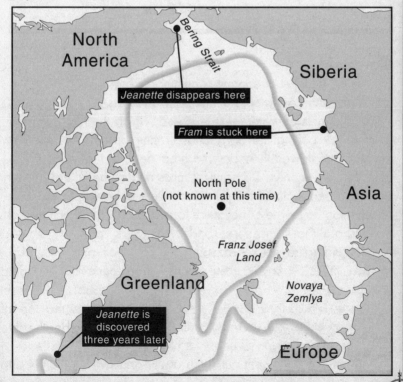

North America

Bering Strait

Siberia

Jeanette disappears here

Fram is stuck here

North Pole (not known at this time)

Asia

Franz Josef Land

Greenland

Novaya Zemlya

Jeanette is discovered three years later

Europe

However, in March 1894, Nansen worked out that the drift was not taking them directly to the North Pole. He therefore decided to leave the *Fram* and, together with one companion, Frederick Johansen, he set off on foot for the Pole (360 nautical miles) and then beyond to Franz Josef Land, a large group of islands north of Russia (1,000 nautical miles away). They had 27 dogs, 3 sledges, 2 kayaks and food for 100 days. Nansen thought the journey would take them four or five months.

Nautical miles

A nautical mile is used for measuring distances at sea and is not the same as a mile measured on land. One nautical mile is equivalent to 1.15 ordinary miles (known as statute miles) or 1.852 km.

Slow work

But the ice was full of enormous hummocks and it soon began to break up as the Arctic spring thawed it. This was very dangerous. Wide channels of water were exposed, which the two men had to cross by putting the dogs and all their possessions into the kayaks. This slowed them down a great deal, so that three weeks later they were only 123 nautical miles nearer the Pole. Nansen and Johansen realized the provisions were not going to last long enough for the journey. They were forced to change direction and make straight for Franz Josef Land.

After many adventures crossing the ice shelf and then 100 nautical miles by kayak, they reached the islands. But by now winter was setting in and Nansen and Johansen had no choice but to stay where they were. They used the native people's skills, building a stone hut, burning walrus blubber for lighting, and killing and skinning polar bears for clothes.

In May 1896 they set out south again and eventually met an

English explorer, Jackson, who arranged a lift home to Norway for them. Nansen and Johansen were very lucky to be alive. They had spent a year and a half living on the ice! They had survived thanks to the skills and techniques of the Arctic peoples.

But what about the *Fram*? Had it been crushed in the ice?

In fact the *Fram*, with its remaining crew, arrived back in Norway just after Nansen, as it had eventually been released from the ice. Nansen was able to meet up with his captain, Sverdrup, a full two and a half years after they had parted company in the pack-ice. Both were regarded as heroes. Adventures aside, they had proved that the Arctic was an ocean with drifting ice on top.

> The later explorer, Amundsen, used the *Fram* on his famous trip to the South Pole. The ship is now in the Norwegian capital of Oslo, where she has been preserved as a museum.

EXTREME FACTS
STUCK IN SEA ICE

Sea ice is formed when the water on the surface of the sea freezes. It can be just a thin covering or, if it is very cold, many metres deep. And the sea can be solid ice for miles and miles. On the edges of the Arctic and Antarctic, sea ice forms in the winter and melts in the summer. Some summers it melts more than others, so some explorers have more luck than others passing through it.

Sea ice is made up of pack-ice (which can move with the currents), fast ice (which is stuck to the shore) and other kinds of ice formations, such as icebergs. The sea ice that the *Fram* was stuck in was 3–4 metres thick and always moving because of the push and pull of the tides, winds and currents. The movement caused the ice to change shape and enormous ridges and hummocks would be created when it was pushed together. Imagine being stuck on a ship for months with just whiteness everywhere. No wonder sailors got bored and depressed, especially if polar bears came sniffing around!

TO THE POLE BY HOT AIR!

One of the next attempts to get to the North Pole was made by hot-air balloon in the 1890s. Remember that aeroplanes did not exist then, but hot-air balloons had been around for over 100 years. A Swedish man called Salomon Andrée persuaded the King of Sweden and others to sponsor his flight. He had a balloon built which he named *Ornen* (Swedish for eagle). Andrée believed that travelling by balloon would solve the problem of going up and down over the hummocks and wide channels of water which had been such a problem for Nansen.

The first attempt to take off failed, but Andrée tried again in July 1897, together with a photographer and an engineer, and succeeded in setting off over the white Arctic! Up, up and away they went ... and they were never seen alive again.

So what happened to them and how do we have this photo of the trip?

Over thirty years after their disappearance, two sailors on a Norwegian seal-hunter happened to find the balloonists' last camp. There they found the *Ornen*'s log book, the men's diaries, some exposed film and one of the bodies in a small boat. The diaries told how the balloon had been wrapped in fog and then weighed down by a film of ice. The *Ornen* had landed on sea ice 300 nautical miles north of Danes Island. From here the balloonists had tried to go on foot over melting ice and wet snow

One of the photographs developed from film found on the Ornen, showing the balloon after it had crash-landed on the sea ice.

but were only able to cover about a kilometre a day. They shot polar bears for food. Eventually, in October 1897, they were too exhausted and weak to go any further. They made their last camp, which was to be found years later.

ON FOOT TO THE POLE

Various people tried to reach the North Pole on foot at the end of the nineteenth century and beginning of the twentieth century. One of the most determined was an American called Robert Peary who spent much of the 1890s travelling and exploring in Greenland. It is said that he was the first to realize that Greenland was an island. In fact, the very northern tip of Greenland is now known as Peary Land.

Like Nansen, while Peary was in Greenland he got to know the local people and their way of living very well. This was all to be of enormous value to him when he became obsessed with the idea of being the first person at the North Pole. And obsessed is what he definitely became.

Arctic peoples

Until recently, many of the people living in the Arctic Circle were known by Europeans as 'Eskimos'. However, increasingly, individual groups are using names that highlight their different ethnic backgrounds, languages and geographical locations. The native people of northern Canada are the Inuit (which means 'people' in their own language). The Inuit used to live in small family groups and move around to hunt and fish. Today they live in towns and work in modern jobs, though they still go on hunting trips. Other native peoples living inside the Arctic Circle include the Alaskan Eskimos, Greenlanders, Saami (formerly known as Lapps) in northern

Scandinavia and western Russia, Nenets in far eastern
Europe and western Asia and the Chuckchi of the
Siberian Arctic.

Huskies
Huskies are not pets, but half-tame working dogs that
are used all around the Arctic Circle by the native
peoples. These dogs can sleep outside in freezing
temperatures for most of the year because their thick,
oily fur keeps out the cold. They also perspire through
their tongues so they are very well suited to this climate.
Other animals, such as the ponies used on Shackleton's
expedition (see page 73–74) are not suitable for the
cold, as they sweat through their bodies. This sweat will
turn into a coating of ice in polar conditions.

Huskies usually work in teams of six or more, pulling a sledge by being hitched to it with harnesses. In this way they can pull heavy loads up to 80 km per day. They can be driven for 18 hours at a time and can reach speeds of over 30 km per hour! In return their handlers need to keep them well fed, usually on a diet of seal meat. However, huskies will eat dog meat. When necessary on long journeys, the native Arctic peoples used to kill the weaker dogs and feed them to the others. Amundsen decided to do this on his trip to the South Pole (see page 79).

From 1898 Peary made various attempts to reach the North Pole – losing eight of his toes to frost-bite on one journey! The toes actually came off his feet when his boots were finally taken off back at base after one of his expeditions ... not a very nice experience. Losing any of your toes means that it becomes very difficult to walk, as it affects your whole balance. But this little problem didn't stop Peary! He said: 'A few toes were not much to give to achieve the Pole.'

EXTREME FACTS
FROSTBITE

Frostbite is something that many polar explorers, past and present, have suffered from. It is an extremely dangerous and unpleasant condition that can result in loss of limbs, fingers, toes – even death.

What is frostbite?
In extreme cold, when tissues of the body become frozen, the nerves are numbed and the blood circulation is cut off.

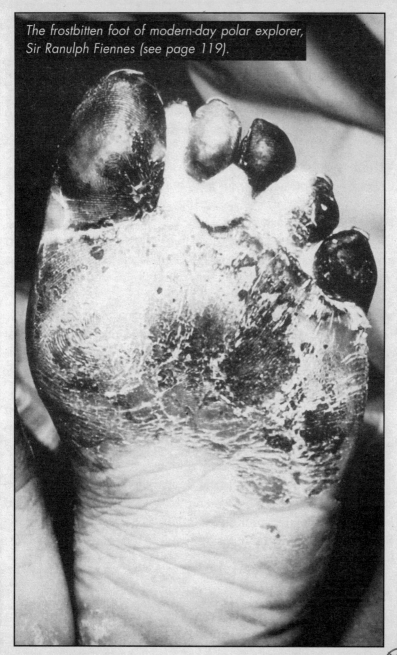

The frostbitten foot of modern-day polar explorer, Sir Ranulph Fiennes (see page 119).

How do you spot it?

White, cold and numb parts of body. Frost-nip is the very early stage of frostbite – the whitening and numbing of the skin. Because you can't feel the frostbitten part of the body early on, it might not be noticed at its treatable stage. However, as the condition progresses, it becomes extremely painful.

Which parts especially?

Outer edges, particularly fingers, ears, nose, cheeks and toes.

How do you treat it?

Warm the area gently. If the frostbite is only mild, the affected part of the body should recover, though it will be very painful as it does so.

What happens if it's really bad?

That part of the body could become infected and poison the rest of the body. Gangrene can result from this (when the body tissue dies and starts decaying). In these cases the only answer is usually to cut off or cut out the infected part.

On the *Endurance* expedition of 1914 (see page 105), a young member of the crew, Blackbarrow, had to have all the toes cut off his left foot because he was so badly frostbitten. The operation took 55 minutes and left him with stumps.

On the Scott expedition to the South Pole in 1911, all the men suffered terribly with frostbite, particularly Captain Oates, who had such agonizing pain in his feet that he could hardly walk. Scott himself realized that losing his right foot would be the least he could hope for. See pages 84–89 for the full story.

Tips

To help prevent frostbite in toes: don't wear boots that are too tight, and leave room to wiggle the toes, which helps keep the circulation going. Peary obviously didn't do this!

Arctic peoples and frostbite

Arctic peoples would wrinkle up their faces now and again to see if there were any stiff patches. If they felt they had a touch of frost-nip they would take a warm hand out of a mitten and place it over the cold numb spot for a couple of minutes. If their toes were affected, they would put their foot on the warm tummy of a travelling companion.

A last attempt

At the age of fifty-two, Peary made his most determined push for the Pole to date. He *was* going to do it this time, he decided, with or without his toes! In July 1908 he left New York with five other Americans on a ship called the *Roosevelt* and landed on the north-west coast of Greenland a month later. The ship collected some local families (49 men, women and children in all) and 246 dogs. Then everyone wintered on board.

So why did Peary need all the native people? Well, he spent all winter preparing for his expedition. The women made traditional clothing and boots for the expedition team, while the men went hunting to provide meat to smoke for the expedition and fat to give heat and light. The men also made sledges and harnesses for the dogs.

On 1 March 1909 Peary left Cape Columbia (at the very north of Ellesmere Island, part of Canada) to set off over the ice for the North Pole. He took with him 21 native Arctic people, 19 sledges, 133 dogs and his long-time polar companion and servant, an African American called Matthew Henson. Peary himself had to be pulled most of the way on a sledge, as he couldn't walk very far with only two toes.

Peary wanted to keep his Pole team as fresh as possible for their journey so he organized teams with dog sledges to go on ahead of him and leave supplies at places on the route to the Pole (called 'depots'), before returning to base camp. This is something that many explorers have done as it means that you do not have to carry all your supplies with you. The supply depots are usually marked by flags.

Peary had chosen to start the journey before winter had finished and while the ice was still firm, though the hours of daylight were very short and the air was bitterly cold. The team battled on, even though some of the ice ridges they had to climb were over 20 metres high! Sometimes the ice would split in front of them and they then had another channel of water to cross or to go round – unless they were lucky and it closed up again. The explorers stayed in igloos at night which were built for them.

EXTREME FACTS
THE PROBLEM OF MELTING ICE

There are pros and cons to setting off before winter has really finished in the Arctic. At the end of winter there is less daylight but the advantage is that the ice is more solid and easier to cross. After about mid April the going can get very difficult because the ice is steadily thawing and breaking up. This means that more and more water channels start opening up, which have to be crossed or gone around.

Also travelling on a frozen ocean means you can be walking and camping on ice that is actually drifting away from the Pole. You could wake up in your tent to find yourself 5 km or more further from the Pole than when you went to sleep!

Note: The problem of ice melting and turning back into sea is one danger explorers on the Antarctic continent do not have to worry about. Oh, and they don't have to worry about polar bears either ... but, on the other hand, they can suffer from altitude sickness while crossing the high mountains or they might fall down a crevasse! Exploring in either end of the world is pretty extreme.

On 1 April, the party reached the final supply store. Peary believed that they were now just 200 km from the Pole. He and Henson set off with four native Arctic men – Iggianguaq, Ukkujaak, Silluk and Oodaaq – as well as dogs and sledges.

Did he ever make the Pole? Listen in ...

On 6 April, Peary's diary reads:

The Pole at last!!! The prize of 3 centuries, my dream and ambition for 23 years. Mine at last.

So, just five days after leaving his last supply depot, 200 km away, he claimed to be standing at the North Pole. It was pretty quick timing!

After spending about thirty hours at what he believed was the Pole (taking bearings and photographs, and sleeping for a while in an igloo), Peary and his team set off back to the *Roosevelt*.

This return journey was also very quick (no, they didn't find the remains of Andrée's balloon and use that!). Peary's party returned to the *Roosevelt* after spending only 19 days crossing 780 km of solid ice, melting ice and snow. Everyone on board the ship celebrated their success.

A long wait

However, the ship was still stuck in the winter ice and Peary had to wait until the summer before it was free. Imagine his sense of frustration as he waited to get to a place from where he could cable the great news to America! As soon as he could, on 5 September, Peary sent a telegram to his wife:

Have made good at last. I have the Pole. Am well. Love.

He arrived in America at the end of September 1909. But Peary did not get the hero's welcome he had expected from his fellow Americans.

The fact was that just days before he had sent the telegram, the *New York Herald* had received a cable from an American doctor, called Frederick Cook, who claimed *he* had reached the North Pole on 21 April 1908 – a whole year before Peary! When Peary heard about this he spent the rest of his life trying to prove that Cook had never reached the North Pole.

Who was Frederick Cook? In fact, Peary knew him well because Cook had been in Greenland with him as expedition doctor in the 1890s. A rich American had financed Cook to try to get to the Pole in 1907–8.

A big row!

The quarrels between the two men became very public and two of the big newspapers got involved. The *New York Times* supported Peary while the *Herald Tribune* backed Cook. Even Congress (the American parliament) debated the issue! Eventually the argument seemed to be settled when in 1911 Congress decided by 135 votes to 34 that Cook had never reached the Pole and that Peary was therefore the winner.

But the questions continued. Neither Cook nor Peary had provided enough information on navigational observations from their journeys to prove their stories exactly. Today many people doubt that either of them actually reached the North Pole!

So how do you know if you are at one of the Poles?

Well, nowadays the South Pole has a marker (though every year this has to be repositioned a metre or two back to its original place to compensate for the shifting ice sheets beneath). However, there is no marker at the North Pole – it wouldn't stay put for long on the drifting sea ice of the Arctic Ocean! At the North Pole, each expedition tends to stick a marker, such as a flag, in the ground for the obligatory photograph, but this will quickly move away afterwards and disappear into the ocean ice.

If you want to check that you are at the North Pole itself, you have to make accurate calculations. This is what early explorers had to do at both the Poles. Nowadays satellite links can help with the calculations that used to be very difficult. There are no distinguishing features on either of the Poles' endless, frozen white horizons. The early explorers had to look at the sun and stars and find their position with a sextant, a special instrument used for measuring angles between distances. But clouds, fog and blizzards mean the sun is not always visible. Compasses are not very useful because they are not reliable so near a magnetic pole (see pages 76–77) and instruments in general tend to freeze up. (Explorers to the Poles today still have this problem.)

It was not easy for extreme explorers 100 years ago to calculate that they were definitely at 90° of latitude, which explains why Peary and Cook may have been mistaken in thinking they had reached the Pole.

So who *was* first to the North Pole, then?

Well, the first people who calculated their position exactly were four Russians who got there by plane, landing on 23 April 1948 – about forty-one years after Peary's claim. The first person who proved that he reached the North Pole overland was an American, Ralph Plaidsted. He arrived there on 20 April 1968 with three companions, having travelled in a motorized sledge called a Skidoo.

However, it cannot be disputed that both Cook and Peary made epic journeys with their teams over the ice and snow – at least, let's give them both credit for that.

ATTEMPT ON THE SOUTH POLE

Well, what was happening on the opposite side of the world while all this was going on in the Arctic?

To begin with, not a lot really!

For about 50 years until the mid 1890s, almost all polar exploration had taken place in the north of the world. So in 1895, in London, the Sixth International Geographical Congress declared:

'The exploration of the Antarctic Regions is the greatest piece of geographical exploration still to be undertaken.'

The countries involved stated that they wanted to work together to make scientific expeditions to the continent of Antarctica. As a result, during the next 20 years, 10 nations sent more than 20 expeditions between them to explore Antarctica. All the explorers had tales to tell of the adventure, the excitement, the fear and, of course, the terrible, terrible cold endured on these trips. Remember that the Antarctic is the coldest place in the entire world, colder even than the Arctic.

These days there are warm cosy permanent bases in Antarctica, with everything from washing-machines to hot showers. But even in these luxurious conditions, people find spending the winter on the bleak continent extremely difficult to cope with. The long months spent in darkness, with little company, can be very lonely and depressing. You can feel as isolated here as an astronaut stranded in space. In fact, NASA (America's National Aeronautics and Space Administration) has done a great deal of research here on the effects of space on humans.

At least nowadays you can communicate with the rest of the world. Imagine what it must have been like for the early adventurers. There was total darkness, no contact with the outside world, and only the same faces day after day – sometimes for years. No wonder that in the 1890s two people went mad on the *Belgica*, the first ship to get trapped in the Antarctic pack-ice for the winter.

CAPTAIN SCOTT AND THE 'DISCOVERY' EXPEDITION

The British National Antarctic Expedition was planned at the end of the nineteenth century. Its leader was Robert Falcon Scott, a naval officer who had no polar experience. However he had greatly impressed one of the key people behind the expedition, Sir Clements Markham, the President of the Royal Geographical Society (RGS).

The RGS decided that a special ship should be built, the first one to be constructed specifically for exploring and for undertaking scientific research in the Antarctic. It would have to be made of wood so it would be flexible in ice and could take magnetic observations. However, by then wooden ships were not being built so often, as new methods of construction were coming into use. So who could build it?

The order was won by the Dundee Shipbuilders Company in Scotland which had been building whaling ships for the Arctic for years and so it had a lot of knowledge about ships for polar regions. By March 1901 the *Discovery* had been finished.

Sponsors

Expeditions to the polar lands were costly affairs and most explorers had to find at least one sponsor – a person or organization – who would pay for them in return for publicity.

Many of the items on board the *Discovery* were supplied by sponsors who still exist, for example:

- Cadbury's provided nearly 2 tons of cocoa powder
- Colman's gave cases of mustard and barrels of flour (9 tons in all)
- Bird & Son donated 8 cwt of custard powder
- Evans, Lesher & Webb provided 156 gallons of tinned lime juice

Other provisions included 150 lb of tinned pheasant, 500 lb of tinned turkey and everything from cherry sauce to Brussels sprouts, marmalade to salt. Not to mention 207 gallons of brandy, 207 gallons of whisky, 28 cases of champagne and 1,800 lb of tobacco!

Among Scott's team was a 26-year-old Merchant Navy officer, born in Ireland, called Ernest Shackleton. Shackleton and Scott were to become two of the most famous names associated with

The Discovery after anchoring in the Antarctic. The men prepare for a skiing race.

Antarctic exploration. This was the first trip to the region for both of them.

The *Discovery*'s crew included many scientists. One of them was Dr Edward 'Bill' Wilson who became great friends with Scott and who was eventually to die with him on the final expedition to the South Pole (see page 91). Wilson was also a keen artist and many of our early drawings of the Antarctic were made by him.

The *Discovery* left Britain amid great excitement and sailed to the Antarctic via New Zealand, anchoring in McMurdo Sound on Ross Island in February 1902. There the crew spent the winter.

Living quarters

The men put up two small observation huts and a larger prefabricated hut which they used for work and recreation, and as a store. The place where it was set up has become known as Hut Point. The team remained living on board the *Discovery*, which was now locked in the ice.

Normal navy life was maintained as much as possible, with the officers and crew living in separate quarters. They even had their main meal of the day at different times – officers at 6 p.m., and the others in the middle of the day. This meal usually consisted of soup, meat and a fruit tart.

Daily tasks

The men filled their days with tasks such as collecting ice for water and making sure all their equipment was kept in a good state – sailors have to be very good at sewing! The men also caught penguins and seals to eat while the scientists carried out their experiments. Some of the penguins were kept, frozen, for tests. Before dissecting them, Dr Wilson used to put them on a shelf above the stove to defrost. It was the warmest place available, but probably not the most pleasant sight for the men huddling around the cosy stove!

Entertainment

The men did a lot of things to keep themselves amused during the evenings – card games, concerts, wood-carving – and they also contributed to their own magazine, the *South Polar Times*. Shackleton was the editor and it was published once a month for the expedition members' entertainment. Shackleton's office was in a coal bunker.

Everybody contributed to the magazine. Items included drawings from Dr Wilson, scientific news, stories about day-to-day tasks, a sports page and some terrible jokes. Now and again the expedition members put on performances in one of the huts. They also played slippery football on the ice!

A very late Christmas party

On 21 June, the men celebrated Christmas. It was a rather odd day to choose, but the group hadn't felt much like celebrating it 6 months before, because one of the crew had been killed falling off the top of the mast as they left New Zealand. Now it seemed like a good idea. They ate Christmas cake and pudding and opened presents from their families, all of which had been brought with them. They started a tradition because this day, now called Midwinter's Day, is still celebrated in Antarctica.

The attempt on the Pole

A lot of scientific work was accomplished around Hut Point, but Scott was also keen to try and make for the South Pole itself, carrying out observations *en route*. On 2 November 1902, as the days began to get lighter, he set out with Shackleton and Wilson on the most daring journey yet to be made in Antarctica. They had 19 dogs, 5 sledges of supplies and estimated that they would be away for two to three months. None of them had much experience of driving dog-sledges, or skiing either – it was a tough way to learn. They faced harsh winds, bitter cold and, in some places, steep ice ridges, up which the dogs could not pull the sledges. Here the men put on harnesses and pulled – literally manhauled – the sledges themselves. After latitude 80° they were entering uncharted terrain, where no human had been before. The team mapped it as they went along. By now the explorers were suffering both mentally and physically.

British explorers came to regard manhauling the sledges as the only true way to travel in Antarctica. They said it was cruel to force the dogs to do this sort of work. However, other explorers, such as Amundsen (who reached the South Pole first – see pages 82–84) used dog-sledges successfully.

Unfortunately, the British team had no real idea how to look after their huskies. As a result, the dogs' conditions worsened and, unfortunately, some of them had to be killed early on in the expedition. They were fed to the others. Then, because there had been problems with pulling the heavy sledges, the explorers decided to throw away some of their supplies, thus reducing their rations. The men were not eating enough for the hard, cold work they were doing and they were so hungry that they dreamt about food constantly. In addition, frostbite, scurvy and snow-blindness were beginning to affect them and tensions rose. Shackleton did not agree with some of Scott's decisions and found it difficult to hide his feelings.

After reaching 82° 17′ on 30 December 1902, fifty-eight days into the journey, the expedition decided to head for home. The return trip was terrible. All the men were ill, especially Shackleton, who was now suffering from serious scurvy and coughing up blood. The remaining dogs were almost useless

This picture shows Shackleton's men dragging, or manhauling, their sledges up the rim of the polar plateau on a later expedition of 1908.

and ended up being hitched behind the sledges that the men were pulling themselves.

After 93 tiring days and having travelled over 1,500 km, the exhausted group arrived back at Hut Point. The expedition had gone further south than any human being before and had got to within 850 km of the South Pole. It was a great achievement, but it had taken its toll on the team.

Although Shackleton began to recover from his scurvy, Scott sent him back to Britain (with seven others) on a relief ship, saying he needed to recuperate. However, Shackleton felt that Scott was looking for an excuse to get rid of him because he had questioned Scott's leadership decisions.

Shackleton vowed he would be back and became obsessed with the idea of being the first man to reach the South Pole. He was later to become one of the most famous polar explorers of all time.

The second winter

With the *Discovery* still trapped in the ice, Scott and the remaining men spent a second winter on the continent (which they had not planned to do). The following spring the relief ships the *Morning* and the *Terra Nova* were sent by the British government to bring them home, with the message that the *Discovery* should be abandoned if she could not be freed. However on 16 February 1904, the ice released her and she was able to sail back to the British Isles.

Scott came home to a hero's welcome. However, he wrote privately:

Wherever my destiny may in future lead me, I hope it will not again be to the interior of the Antarctic continent.

But Shackleton's plans were to change his mind ...

EXTREME FACTS
SNOW-BLINDNESS AND SUNBURN

Snow-blindness
Snow-blindness can be caused by looking at dazzling snow-white landscapes. The bright glare of the snow and ice means you can get snow-blindness even on an overcast day in the polar regions.

Symptoms?
- Very painful eyes that itch horribly as if full of grit, weep and become red.
- Bad headaches
- In extreme cases, it is even possible to become temporarily blind, hence the name.

How do you avoid it?
Explorers need to wear special goggles to protect their eyes.
In the Arctic the native peoples traditionally wore wooden goggles with a very narrow slit to protect the eyes from the glare.

On Scott's expedition, Dr Wilson suffered badly from snow-blindness because he was always taking his goggles off to sketch. He ended up having to haul his sledge wearing a blindfold while Scott described the landscape to him.

Sunburn
Sunburn is a problem in the polar regions too! Like snow-blindness it is caused by the sun reflecting off the ice, the snow and the sea.

SHACKLETON SETS OFF AGAIN

Shackleton became determined to reach the South Pole before Scott. In 1907 he managed to persuade a rich industrialist, William Beardmore, to put up the initial sponsorship for a new expedition. Beardmore was later rewarded when Shackleton named a newly discovered Antarctic glacier after him.

On New Year's Day 1908 Shackleton and his team of sixteen left New Zealand in a little 40-year-old sealer (a boat used for hunting seals) called *Nimrod*. Douglas Mawson, a geologist, was one of three scientists on board (see page 94).

Dogs v. Ponies

Against Nansen's advice, Shackleton decided to rely on ponies rather than dogs. This was to prove a foolish move because ponies are totally unsuited to Antarctic conditions. Not only do they sink in deep snow but they sweat all over their bodies, and in freezing conditions the sweat turns to ice. Also, unlike huskies, they cannot sleep outside in blizzard conditions. Shackleton decided on ponies because he worked out that they could pull more than dogs. He calculated that a pony pulls 800 kg and eats 5 kg a day, while a dog can only pull 50 kg and needs 750 g.

Scott had extracted a promise from Shackleton that his expedition would not base itself at McMurdo Sound because Scott felt that was his territory. However, Shackleton was forced to set up his camp on McMurdo Sound since ice blocked his entry to the Bay of Whales. It is said that Scott never forgave him.

First book published in Antarctica

Shackleton planned to print an illustrated account of the expedition while on the continent itself. A printing press and an etching press were lent to him by the British firm of Joseph

---

Carston & Sons and some of the men received lessons in using them before they left England. In the book, *Aurora Australis*, they described the conditions they worked under:

The temperature varies; it is too cold to keep the printer's ink fluid; it gets sticky and freezes. To cope with this a candle was set burning underneath the plate on which the ink was. This was alright but it made the ink too fluid, and the temperature had to be regulated by moving the candle about.

After wintering in McMurdo Sound, Shackleton and three men set off with four ponies to try to reach the Pole. The other six ponies had already died. Therefore the men had to pull some of the sledges themselves. They took with them rations of 900 g of pemmican and biscuits per person per day.

The men discovered the monstrous heights of the enormous 200 km Beardmore Glacier and proceeded to climb up it. They had a terrible time. The glacier was full of ridges and dangerous crevasses and the men did not have any proper mountaineering equipment. They slipped and slithered their way through the ice and slushy snow, sometimes up to their knees, knowing that one accidental slip into a crevasse could mean death. They continued on until, on 9 January 1909, the seventieth day after they had left McMurdo Sound, they decided to turn back. The men were shattered and they were running low on food. It was a huge disappointment, since they were only 180 km away from the Pole. However, their lives were now at stake. Shackleton later said to his wife, Emily: 'A live donkey is better than a dead lion, isn't it?'

The return journey took fifty days during which time one of the men, Marshall, became very ill and had to be left behind in a tent with another man to look after him. Shackleton and his colleague Wild continued on, but when they arrived back at base, a

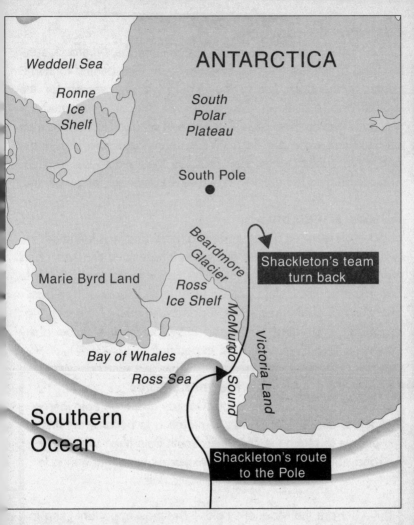

Weddell Sea

Ronne
Ice
Shelf

ANTARCTICA

South
Polar
Plateau

South Pole

Beardmore Glacier

Shackleton's team
turn back

Marie Byrd Land

Ross
Ice Shelf

McMurdo Sound

Victoria Land

Bay of Whales

Ross Sea

Southern
Ocean

Shackleton's route
to the Pole

terrible sight confronted them. The *Nimrod* was no longer there! It was 28 February. Shackleton was in despair. He had told the *Nimrod*'s captain to leave by 1 March in case she got trapped in ice, but he had hoped they would have waited until the last moment. In fact, the captain had left because he thought Shackleton's party must be dead.

Last-minute reprieve

Luckily for the very much alive Shackleton, the *Nimrod*'s crew decided at the last moment to leave some men behind to spend winter in the base hut so they could go and search for the expedition's bodies in the spring. As the ship returned on 1 March to drop them off, the crew were amazed to see two men on Hut Point waving a flag. Words cannot describe Shackleton and Wild's relief when they realized they would be rescued. Shackleton then led a party to rescue the two men left in the tent.

A hero's welcome

Shackleton returned home a national hero and was knighted. He was only thirty-six. He had proved that he valued the lives of his men before anything else, even his ambition to reach the Pole first. His leadership skills gained him the nickname of 'The Boss'. Shackleton's ability to get the support and trust of his men was probably his greatest skill – and this would prove to be vitally important on his next Antarctic expedition.

The Magnetic Poles

In 1909, David, Mawson and Mackay made an epic journey across almost 1,600 km of Antarctica to become the first people to reach the Magnetic South Pole (then in Victoria Land). Since then many other explorers have made trips to reach the Magnetic Poles.

But what are the Magnetic Poles? The most important thing to remember is that they are not the same as the Geographic Poles. These are fixed in one place – where lines of longitude meet at the top and bottom of the globe (see page 14). However, the Magnetic Poles are always drifting slowly, moving about 10–15 km per year due to the effect of the earth's orbit. The reason why these Poles exist is because the earth acts like a giant magnet with its own north and south poles lined up on its magnetism. Explorers using a magnetic compass will find it points to the Magnetic Poles.

At the moment the Magnetic North Pole is in northern Canada, about 1,000 km from the Geographic North Pole. The Magnetic South Pole is in the sea on the Australian side of the Antarctic continent.

Captain James Clark Ross was the first person to reach the Magnetic North Pole, in 1831.

THE RACE IS ON!

Scott was resentful of Shackleton's knighthood. He set about organizing another expedition because he was determined to place the British flag on the South Pole.

But the British navy was not as keen to support him now since there were rumours of a possible war in Europe. Scott decided to use *The Times* newspaper to ask the public for support.

Money was raised, but not enough to build a special ship. In fact Scott used the *Terra Nova* (meaning *New Land*), one of the two relief ships that had collected his last expedition. This ship was an old Scottish whaler and conditions were very cramped on the journey from Britain to Antarctica. A long, hard journey is not a good mental or physical start to a tough expedition.

THE ADVENTURE BEGINS

Scott left London in June 1910, with 65 men, 17 ponies, 30 dogs and 3 motorized sledges. In 1909 news of both Peary and Cook's claims to the North Pole had been announced. Scott wrote :

What matters now, is that the Pole should be obtained by an Englishman.

Scott had no idea that he was at the starting-line of a very serious race. Unknown to almost everybody, a very formidable competitor had also just left the starting blocks in his own country. His aim was to race against Scott.

The Amundsen challenge

Remember Roald Amundsen? He was definitely a man who was into polar travel. He and his crew of four were the first to sail the North-west Passage (see page 39). In 1909 he was making preparations to be the first man to the North Pole when he was devastated to hear that Peary and Cook had already claimed it.

So he decided to go south and become the first man to stand at the South Pole. But he didn't tell anyone and carried on pretending he was still going to the North Pole. It was only when he got to Madeira, an island off the coast of Africa, that he informed his crew members and offered those who didn't want to continue the opportunity to go home. But they all said they wanted to stay with him. He sent Scott a telegram, and wrote to the King of Norway and Nansen. The telegram to Scott let him know his plans:

Beg leave to inform you proceeding Antarctic.

Scott was furious when he heard.

Getting ready for the race

In January 1911 Amundsen landed in the Bay of Whales and set up a base on the Ross Ice Shelf, with 8 companions and 116 dogs. In the next weeks of fading light, until the end of March, the party set up supply depots *en route* to the Pole. These contained food, fuel, cooking stoves, matches, sleeping bags and clothes. The party spent the winter preparing and re-examining everything for the attempt on the Pole. Amundsen was particularly keen to make sure the dogs were well fed and kept fit and healthy. He felt the huskies were the key to the success of his expedition.

Scott landed in McMurdo Sound in January, one week before Amundsen. Scott made his base at Cape Evans on Ross Island, about 650 km west of Amundsen. Scott too set up supply depots *en route* to the Pole before winter. During the winter, his fifteen scientists carried out research.

Sweating in the cold

You might think that in a freezing climate, piling on more clothes to keep warm is the answer. This is not the case. The hard work and heavy hauling of a polar expedition soon leaves you soaked in sweat. If the sweat cannot evaporate, it freezes.

On Scott's expedition many of the men's clothes were made of wool and cotton. Like most Europeans of the time they had the ends of their clothes sealed to keep out the snow and freezing cold. They did not realize that this was actually making things worse for them. The fact that they did not wear layers that they could adjust easily, combined with manhauling their sledges, increased their problems. The exercise caused them to sweat a lot. The sweat then froze into ice, making their clothes very uncomfortable, heavy ... and even colder.

At night, when the men were warming up in their sleeping bags, the ice melted, completely soaking their clothes and bags, and then froze again when they got up in the morning. They did not have any fuel to dry out the clothes properly in the tent.

Amundsen's team wore clothes based on what the native Arctic people wore, mainly layers of furs. The layers allowed the air to circulate and stopped the sweat building up, so

> *they did not suffer from the problems of Scott's team.*
>
> *Most Europeans of the time also wore hoods separately from their waterproof canvas jackets, which meant that the icy wind just cut into the backs of their necks, making their misery even worse. However, most expeditions of the time did use fur boots and fur sleeping bags.*

The first Antarctic winter journey

In the midst of the Antarctic winter, 27 June 1911 (just after the base Midwinter's Day party), three members of Scott's expedition set off to look for the eggs of the Emperor penguin to take back to London to study. These men (Edward Wilson, 'Birdie' Bowers and Apsley Cherry-Garrard) were the first people ever to make an attempt to travel during the terrible Antarctic winter, in 24-hour darkness. They trekked to Cape Crozier, about 100 km away, in temperatures that were as low as –60°C. They suffered from ice forming inside their clothes and their sleeping bags. They had some terrible moments, the worst being when their tent blew away in a blizzard. Without shelter they would have died in those conditions. But, miraculously, they found the tent near by two days later, when the storm ended. This saved their lives.

In spite of these almost impossible hardships, the team managed to bring back three penguin eggs to the base hut (two others were broken). When they returned on 1 August their frozen clothes literally had to be cut from their bodies.

When he returned to England, Cherry-Garrard took the eggs to the Natural History Museum in London. He later wrote:

I do not believe anybody on earth has a worse time than an Emperor penguin.

Wilson and Bowers were to accompany Scott to the Pole and die with him eight months later.

Emperor penguins

Emperor penguins are unusual because it is the male that protects the one large egg his mate has laid. During the Antarctic winter the female goes off to fatten up, ready to feed her chick when it hatches. The male keeps the egg warm under a special flap between his feet. He huddles together with the other males for protection from the terrible, freezing blizzards. The male penguins stand in groups of thousands in the dark, each doing his turn at the back to block the wind before moving to the front. They spend two whole months like this, getting thinner and thinner as they carry out their duty.

Amundsen sets off

Amundsen set out for the pole on 20 October with a team of four: a dog-handler, a sledge-driver, a ski champion and a whale harpooner! They were all experienced men in ice and snow. They had 4 sledges and 48 dogs.

Although Amundsen's base camp was nearer to the Pole than Scott's, he was travelling on a new route. He did not know if there were mountains in his way. He was, however, convinced that dogs could pull sledges up mountains, while Scott was not.

On 17 November the group reached the bottom of a rugged mountain range and Amundsen was proved right. After five arduous days of climbing across the dangerous crevasses of the Axel Heiberg Glacier (which they named after a Norwegian sponsor), the dogs managed to reach the top with their sledges. Here the men killed 24 of the weaker dogs as planned and fed them to the others. Amundsen called this place 'The Butcher's Shop'.

On to the Pole!

They continued on over more crevasses and glaciers, through

terrible weather conditions, blizzards and thick fog. As they were now travelling at high altitude, this added to their problems by making breathing difficult. They kept a constant look out for Scott, worried that his expedition might be somewhere close. As they neared the Pole the altitude began to decrease and on 14 December Amundsen and his team reached 90°S – the Pole itself! There was no sign of Scott.

They were the first men ever to get to this desolate place.

The group spent a couple of days at the South Pole, where they carefully measured the altitude of the sun with a special instrument called a sextant. This was something neither Cook nor Peary had done. Amundsen was determined that no one was going to challenge his claim of having reached the South Pole. They also planted the Norwegian flag and pitched a tent (with messages, spare clothes and equipment) at the spot where they calculated the Pole was. They set up black marker flags around it.

In the tent Amundsen left a letter for Scott together with one for the King of Norway, in case he and his group died on the return journey. He set off on 17 January, writing in his diary:

Farewell, dear Pole, I don't think we'll meet again.

They now had 16 dogs and 2 sledges. They were still reasonably fit and knew they had food waiting in well-marked depots. They reached their base hut, on 25 January 1912, having been away for 99 days.

Amundsen's letter to Scott

Dear Captain Scott,
As you are probably the first to reach this area

after us, I will ask you kindly to forward this letter to King Haakon VII. If you can use any of the articles left in the tent, please do not hesitate to do so. With kind regards. I wish you a safe return.

Yours truly,

Roald Amundsen.

Scott sets off

Scott's expedition set off two weeks after Amundsen, on 24 November 1911, from his base camp at McMurdo Sound. He had 16 men, 2 motorized sledges, 12 other sledges, 23 Siberian huskies and 10 ponies from north China.

A bad start

The support team were to peel off and turn back as the main expedition advanced. The motorized sledges proved unreliable, finally breaking down after 80 km due to the intense cold. The poor ponies had to be shot after crossing the Ross Ice Shelf. They were exhausted, covered in frozen sweat and it would have been cruel to force them on any further. On 10 December, as planned, the dogs were sent back at the foot of the Beardmore Glacier. Scott assumed the dogs would never be able to pull the sledges up it.

Three teams of four men each pulled a sledge up the huge glacier. It was a very tough eleven-day climb and they encountered huge crevasses. One of the men fell in, but was lucky enough to be held by his harness and pulled out by the others. Little did they know that Amundsen had reached the Pole while they were climbing.

At the top of the glacier Scott sent back the rest of the support team, but added one more man to his final Pole party, Bowers. This was an unwise decision since the supplies had been planned only for four men. Also Bowers had no skis, so he sank into the deep snow as he walked. The other members of the team were Wilson, Oates and Evans.

The manhauling was exhausting work. Soon the men were beginning to show the early signs of scurvy and shortage of food, but they still continued to drag the sledges behind them. On 9 January 1912 they passed Shackleton's southernmost point of three years before.

The Worst happens

On 16 January, as they neared the Pole, a terrible sight greeted them. They saw a flag fluttering in the distance.

Scott's diary says:

The worst has happened, or nearly the worst . . . The Norwegians have forestalled us and are first at the Pole . . . Tomorrow we must march onto the Pole and then hasten home with all the speed we can command.

The Norwegians had beaten them to the end of the earth by only thirty-three days.

The men's intense disappointment can been seen in the group photograph taken at the Pole. The expedition photographer, Ponting, had given them instructions on how to use the camera. Wilson made some sketches of the polar landscape as he always did at any stop. The undeveloped film and the sketches were later found among the dead men's things in their tent. Scott wrote in his diary:

The Pole, yes, but under very different circumstances to those expected . . . Great God! this is an awful place . . .

What should have been a triumphant moment turns to misery and disappointment as Scott and his men photograph themselves at the South Pole. Captain Scott is in the centre holding the Union flag.

Return journey

The five men set off to struggle back on the 1,500-km journey to their base camp. They were already weak, exhausted and undernourished as they left the Pole. They had used up a lot of energy pulling their sledges to this point. Now their morale was low after finding out that they had lost the race. They had to summon up every last ounce of energy they had left to try and get home. Amundsen's team had not been so exhausted at this point because the dogs had been pulling the sledges.

All the men were now suffering badly. In addition to the very hard work of manhauling, they were having trouble finding their supply depots. The flags that marked them were not very clear in the polar landscape and the men wasted valuable time and energy looking for them. They *had* to find them, however, because their limited rations were running very low. They were short on fuel for cooking too.

Evans dies

Frostbite, snow-blindness and scurvy were beginning to take their toll. Evans, a large Welshman, had not been well for a while and was completely spent. His hands were badly frost-bitten and the others suspected that he was having a breakdown. After a fall at the foot of the Beardmore Glacier, on 17 February, he collapsed and never recovered. He was the first of Scott's team to die.

Gallant Oates

Captain Oates was also suffering badly from frostbite. He was trying hard to keep it to himself despite the terrible pain in his feet. It is also likely that an old war wound on his leg had reopened – scurvy can make scars from years before rip apart.

Oates had been in extreme pain for weeks before he eventually told the others. By this time the frostbite in his feet had developed into gangrene and it was very difficult for him to walk. Poor Oates was very worried that he was slowing down the party. He insisted that they go on without him, but they refused to leave him behind.

A terrible sacrifice

One night, Oates went to sleep hoping that he would never wake up, but, to his intense misery, he did. He then struggled

This famous painting shows Captain Oates sacrificing his life to the terrible blizzard. No wonder it is called 'A Very Gallant Gentleman'.

out of the tent into a blizzard, apparently with the famous words, 'I am just going outside and may be some time.'

It was 17 March, the day of his thirty-second birthday. He was never seen again.

Oates's memorial
Oates's death is commemorated every year at a church service held by his regiment, the Royal Dragoon Guards. This is the only British regiment to honour a soldier who died in peacetime.

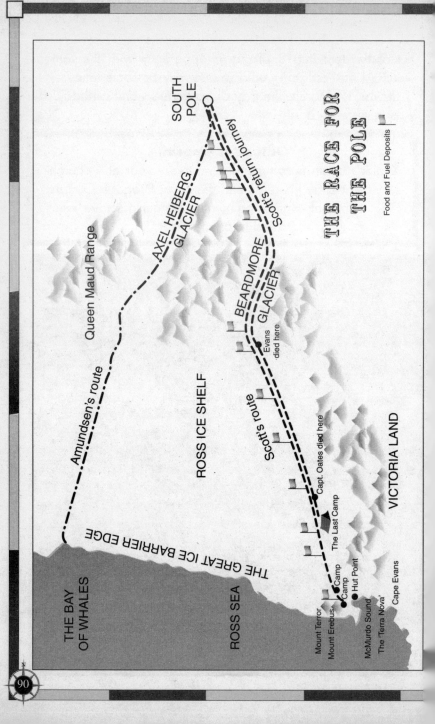

THE RACE FOR THE POLE

SOUTH POLE

AXEL HEIBERG GLACIER

Queen Maud Range

Amundsen's route

BEARDMORE GLACIER

Scott's return journey

ROSS ICE SHELF

Scott's route

Evans died here

Capt. Oates died here

THE BAY OF WHALES

THE GREAT ICE BARRIER EDGE

ROSS SEA

The Last Camp

Camp

Camp

Hut Point

Mount Terror

Mount Erebus

McMurdo Sound

The 'Terra Nova'

Cape Evans

VICTORIA LAND

Food and Fuel Deposits

N

The end approaches

Scott, Wilson and Bowers had to struggle on. By 21 March they knew they were within 17 km of the next supply depot. Even though they were so close, they were never to make it. Their diaries and writings record how they were pinned in the tent for four days by a terrible blizzard while their fuel and food ran down. Scott's last diary entry was dated 29 March. He wrote:

Every day we have been ready to start for our depot 11 miles away, but outside the door of the tent it remains a scene of whirling drift. I do not think we can hope for any better things now. We shall stick it out to the end, but we are getting weaker, of course, and the end cannot be far. It seems a pity, but I do not think I can write more.

The three bodies in the snow-buried green tent were discovered the following November by a search party. They also found Scott's diary, the undeveloped film from the Pole, Wilson's sketches and, on a nearby sledge, Amundsen's letter to the King of Norway. There were also 16 kg of rocks on the sledge. Scott was keen to the end to prove that this was a scientific expedition. The search party made a cross out of skis and then left the bodies in the tent to be covered up by the snow again.

EXTREME FACTS
DANGEROUS SNOW

Very little snow falls in Antarctica. **Blizzards** here are caused when strong winds pick up the surface snow and blow it wildly around. Blizzards can last for days. Whirling walls of snow close in on you from every direction, a thundering noise (like the sea in a terrible storm) sounds in your ears, you feel as though you are suffocating and it is hard to breathe. It's impossible to speak and impossible to see. Blizzards can be completely disorientating and people can easily get lost only a few footsteps away from the door of their base hut. They are very dangerous and so it is best to stay inside when one blows up.

White-outs are also very dangerous. These occur when the sky is overcast – everything looks the same, just white, or whitish-grey. This means there is no sign of the horizon and you can't see where the sky stops and the ground begins. There are no shadows, so nothing has any sense of depth. It is very frightening to be in the middle of a white-out, as it is like being inside an optical illusion. What appears to be a flat area could be a dip, or a big hill could just be a little bump. Explorers can only stumble around and can easily get lost, aeroplanes crash – and even birds lose their sense of perspective and fly straight into the ground.

Amundsen and Scott – the aftermath

At the beginning of 1912 the whole world knew about Amundsen's incredible achievement. It was not until November that the bodies of Scott and his party were discovered and the news did not reach the outside world until February 1913. Ironically it was Scott who became the great hero, rather than Amundsen! Scott's diaries and his final letters from the tent contributed to his heroic status. In fact he was probably a better writer than leader. His 'Message to the Public' said:

We are weak, writing is difficult, but for my own sake I do not regret this journey, which has shown that Englishmen can endure hardships, help one another, and meet death with as great a fortitude as ever in the past ... Had we lived I should have had a tale to tell of the hardihood, endurance, and courage of my companions which would have stirred the heart of every Englishman. These rough notes and our dead bodies must tell the tale ...

In support of Scott, British newspapers tried to make out that Amundsen had cheated. One of the reasons they gave was that his men hadn't pulled their sledges, like Scott's team. It appeared that Amundsen had had too easy a time of it to suit the British! What they overlooked was the fact that with proper use of skis and dogs the Norwegians had been able to travel much further and much faster than Scott's men. The fact that Amundsen's planning was better than Scott's had been ignored.

Another reason why Scott's image became very important to the public was that during the First World War (1914–18) the story of Scott's heroic suffering for the glory of his country was told to English troops in the trenches of France. When Scott's wife died, letters were found among her things from soldiers saying that Scott's writings had helped them to face the nightmare sufferings and horrific hardships of the war.

EXTREME EXPEDITIONS

FREEZE

CREVASSE CRISIS

One of the big problems of travelling in Antarctica is the constant threat of crevasses. Out of nowhere explorers can suddenly find themselves hurtling hundreds, maybe thousands, of metres down a massive gap in the ice. They are a huge risk.

On Douglas Mawson's expedition to Antarctica, the crevasse threat became all too real. Mawson was an Australian geologist who had first visited Antarctica on Shackleton's 1907–9 *Nimrod* expedition. Mawson then decided to lead his own expedition to explore the Antarctic coast just south of Australia. He and his party of eighteen men set off from Tasmania on 2 December 1911 in an old seal-hunting ship called the *Aurora*.

This expedition had the use of a modern piece of technology – the radio; its first time in Antarctica. There was to be a radio on the expedition ship and one at the main base, at Cape Dennison on Commonwealth Bay. This position was to prove problematic, however, as it turned out to be one of the windiest places in the world! Mawson later called it 'the home of the blizzard'.

The winds were so fierce that often the men had to crawl along on their hands and knees to carry out their daily tasks, or even wiggle along on their stomachs when it got really severe. Even on some of the better days, they had to walk along leaning heavily into the strong wind, always aware that it might suddenly drop and send them crashing heavily to the ground.

EXTREME FACTS
POLAR WINDS

Wind chill

The stronger the wind, the more quickly a human loses heat. For example, a person in −10°C facing a wind moving at 10 km/h can lose as much heat as a person in calm air of −70°C. Modern-day explorer Sir Ranulph Fiennes says that one of the biggest dangers for humans in Antarctica is the wind because every additional knot in its speed makes the human body drop one degree in temperature.

Katabatic winds

Antarctica has the strongest winds in the world. They are called katabatic winds (meaning 'down-flowing') and they occur along the coast. Katabatic winds are caused by colder, denser air rushing down from the higher interior of the continent (the polar plateau) to the coast. They can be as fast as 320 km/h and often come in wild short gusts. These are horrendous conditions to try to work or travel in – in fact almost impossible. Tents can be ripped completely to pieces by a katabatic gust.

Antarctic meteorites

The Mawson expedition made various sledging trips and found the first Antarctic meteorite. Since then, the vast majority of world meteorite finds have been in Antarctica – scientists love hunting for them here as they are likely to be successful!

A terrible end ...

Mawson's expedition is most remembered for the traumas of the three-man sledging party that set out to explore far to the east of their base. The members were Ninnis (a British officer), Mertz (a Swiss ski champion), both expert dog-sledge drivers, and Mawson himself.

It was on 14 December 1912 that disaster struck.

Mertz was walking in front, followed by Mawson then Ninnis. The first two men carefully crossed a snowbridge over a crevasse. Then Mawson noticed Mertz looking puzzled. Mertz was looking back, in the direction of Ninnis. Mawson turned and looked behind him. There was no one else there on the empty white landscape. Ninnis and his dogs and his sledge had completely disappeared from sight.

Horrified, Mertz and Mawson realized that their companion must have fallen through the fragile snowbridge into the crevasse that they had both just crossed. As they hurried back they hoped beyond hope that Ninnis and his six dogs had somehow been wedged by their harness and were hanging just out of sight.

But as Mawson peered over the dangerous edge of the crevasse into the icy nothingness, he could see no sign of his colleague. About 40 metres down, an injured dog was lying on a ledge, whimpering in fear and pain. Terrified, Mawson called his friend's name, but no answer came back. The crevasse was so deep he could not even see its bottom.

For the next three hours Mertz and Mawson lay on the cracked edge of the crevasse, calling again and again into the darkness of the frozen pit until they were hoarse. Eventually they had to come to the terrible conclusion that they would never see their friend Ninnis again, that this enormous icy abyss was to be his grave.

It was to prove to be a double tragedy for the two remaining

Peering into the yawning crevasse, the explorer, Mawson, desperately tries to see some sign of his colleague.

men. Not only had their companion fallen into the gaping crevasse, so had his dogs and sledge. Ninnis had had the stronger dogs. On his sledge had been the men's tent, most of their food and all the dogs' food. Could the two remaining men survive?

Desperate measures

Mawson and Mertz eventually had to come to terms with the seriousness of their situation. Ninnis was dead and they were 500 km from base with no tent and only ten days' worth of food.

It had taken them five weeks to get here. How could they now survive on the return journey?

They were forced to construct a makeshift shelter for themselves by draping a spare tent cover over a broken bit of sledge and Mertz's skis. They fed the six dogs that were left with old boots, gloves and leather straps and tried to make their own rations last by boiling old food bags to make a thin soup.

The two men then set off to struggle against the elements in the direction of their base hut. In desperation for food, they killed and ate the remaining six dogs, finding the livers easiest to chew. They did not know that eating the livers could poison you. A while later, Mertz began to behave very strangely – even biting off part of his badly frostbitten finger. He is likely to have got vitamin A poisoning from the livers, just as Barents and his men had done in 1597 (see page 23). Mertz got more and more ill. Mawson had to pull him along on the sledge, until he died after a sudden fit.

The only survivor

Mawson was at his wits' end. He had lost his two companions and was now totally alone, 160 km from base. And his body seemed to be falling apart – his hair was coming out, he had frost-bite in his toes and fingers and he had to keep the skin of the soles of his feet on with bandages and six pairs of socks! (He was also suffering from vitamin A poisoning.) But he was determined to try and get back to base. He felt he had to achieve this, because he was the leader of the whole expedition. To make his journey less difficult he sawed his sledge in half with a pocket knife to make it lighter.

He set off, painfully and slowly dragging his sledge behind him. It was difficult to keep any sense of hope with no humans or animals for company, just the ice, snow and wailing winds. On one occasion the snow gave way underneath him and he himself fell into a crevasse! Panicking, he thought he too was going to plunge to the icy depths below and suffer as horrendous a death as Ninnis. But his luck held out and his sledge got trapped on the top, with his harness holding him dangling over the gaping hole. He knew at any moment the sledge might go tumbling down below, with him, but he gingerly climbed up his 3-metre rope and managed to scramble on to the firmer ice above the hole. He was alive, but the whole experience had been terrifying.

A life-saver

Mawson had been travelling for twenty-one days on his own and had almost given up on many occasions when, 50 km from the hut, he found something which probably saved his life – a food dump. It had been left by a search party only a few hours earlier. Mawson had been on the verge of dying from starvation before he found it. He could not believe it when he saw the supplies. It was this final boost which gave him the energy to struggle on to the hut.

His last hope

On 1 February he climbed the hill behind his base, he was nearly back to safety now. But an awful sight met his eyes. *Aurora*, his expedition ship, was sailing away without him! Mawson stared in disbelief. After all he had gone through, he had just not made it in time and he was going to be left here alone in the Antarctic to die. This was probably the worst moment of his life.

But what he didn't know was that although the *Aurora* had just sailed (to avoid the winter ice), a team of six men had been left behind in case Mawson's expedition turned up. In complete despair Mawson staggered on to the hut for shelter. Here he was, at last, spotted. But now he was so thin – he had lost half his original weight – that the first person to see him was not able to recognize which of the three men he was, '*Which are you?*' were the first words Mawson heard.

Mawson told the terrible story of what had happened to him and the others. The ship was called back by radio but gales stopped her returning. Mawson and the six men spent a further winter at the base camp. By the time they were picked up in the spring Mawson had recovered from his horrendous ordeal – but he would never forget his friends.

For the rest of his life Mawson believed that the only reason he had not gone down the same crevasse as Ninnis was because he had been sitting on his sledge rather than walking along with it. His weight had been distributed over a wider area than the concentrated weight of Ninnis. He had had an extremely lucky escape.

EXTREME FACTS
CREVASSES

A crevasse is a deep and, seemingly, bottomless crack in the ice. It can be anything from a few millimetres wide to 30 or more metres across. Antarctic explorers have talked about some that are big enough to swallow a whole ship or a double-decker bus!

A crevasse is created when the ice splits and breaks apart as it moves over hidden rocks or downhill. It is often concealed by snow, so you don't know it is there. You can cross a crevasse on a snowbridge if the snow is strong enough to take your weight. But, in the case of Ninnis, his sledge piled with supplies and equipment proved too heavy. Crevasses are a dreadful risk for all expeditions, past and present.

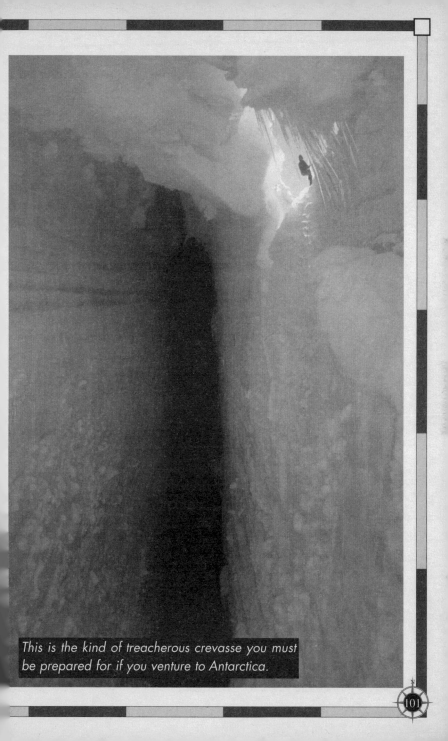

This is the kind of treacherous crevasse you must be prepared for if you venture to Antarctica.

MONSTER HOLES!

Modern-day explorer Sir Ranulph Fiennes describes crevasses as 'monster holes'.

We were on a flat stretch, with not the least sign of an undulation, when I found myself suddenly shooting downwards. I flung both arms out, ski-sticks flailing. My descent stopped short at my armpits. I felt my legs involuntarily treading air, swimming on the void. Gingerly I tried to turn my neck to look backwards at the sledge. My greatest fear at that moment was that it too would break through the thin trapdoor and, like Ninnis, I would cartwheel downwards to snap my spine or crack open my skull on some sharp icy ledge below.

A member of one of Scott's expeditions also wrote about crevasses:

I still dream about them. I loathe them. You never knew when you would be dropping into some bottomless pit, or rushing to help some companion who had disappeared. Coming back down the Beardmore Glacier a man on our sledge went down headfirst, another fell 8 times in 25 minutes. He looked pretty dazed. Always as you fell you wondered if your harness would hold, and you waited for the sudden jerk.

Present-day explorer Dr Mike Stroud, on falling into a crevasse:

> At that moment I was sure I was going to meet my death
> ... I had seen the bottomless pit.
>   I was wrong. Instead of plummeting into the darkness, I
> dropped another ten feet or so before I landed hard on a
> surface, my back crushing painfully into the front of my
> sledge. For a moment I lay still, winded, confused,
> scarcely able to believe my luck. Then I looked around,
> not daring to move, trying to assess my situation. I was
> perched on a narrow snow platform where the crevasse
> had been choked by drift. It was about 20 feet down and
> the walls of shimmering blue rose vertically above me. To
> either side, just a few feet away the crevasse was open
> and the same walls went on down darker and darker until
> they passed out of sight. The blackness beckoned ... my
> platform was horribly thin. It was a precarious position
> and I gazed up at the band of sky, wondering how to get
> out.

Stroud *did* manage to get out with the help of his
companion, Sir Ranulph Fiennes, and a rope which Fiennes
had tied tightly to a sledge at the top. Fiennes pulled on the
rope while Stroud scrambled up the icy side of the crevasse.
Stroud was lucky to be alive. He and Fiennes then went on
to cross the Antarctic continent (see page 119)!

THE BIG
EXTREME EXPEDITIONS
FREEZE

SHACKLETON – THE GREAT LEADER

Now that the South Pole had finally been reached, Shackleton set his sights on another achievement: crossing the whole of the Antarctic continent. He wanted to travel from the Weddell Sea to the Ross Sea via the South Pole, a distance of 3,300 km. He planned to allow 120 days for this journey, which would be called the Imperial Transantarctic Expedition. It was a very, very ambitious idea.

SHACKLETON'S 'ENDURANCE' ADVENTURE

His plan was to have two ships and two groups, one for each side of the continent. One ship was to land the expedition party itself on the Weddell Sea side. The other ship was to take a party to the Ross Sea side. From here the men would set up supply bases on the other side of the Pole for the crossing group to use. It is said that Shackleton advertised for men to join the expedition with the following words:

**Men wanted for Hazardous Journey.
Small wages, bitter cold, long months of
complete darkness, constant danger,
safe return doubtful.**

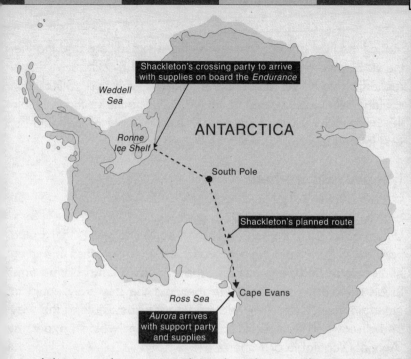

Shackleton's crossing party to arrive with supplies on board the *Endurance*

Weddell Sea

ANTARCTICA

Ronne Ice Shelf

South Pole

Shackleton's planned route

Ross Sea

Cape Evans

Aurora arrives with support party and supplies

It didn't sound too appealing, but those with the spirit of adventure were prepared to put up with these conditions in return for the sense of achievement and the glory a successful trip would reward them with.

Shackleton's preparations took a year and one of his ships, the *Endurance*, was built specially. In August 1914 he was ready to go. But, just as he was about to leave Britain, the First World War broke out. Shackleton felt that he must offer his ships and men for the war. However, he was told to go on. It was thought the expedition would be good for national morale. The two ships, *Aurora* and *Endurance*, sailed off for different parts of the Antarctic continent.

During the voyage a stowaway was found hiding in a locker. He was 19-year-old Percy Blackbarrow, a young man who had (unsuccessfully) tried to join the expedition party in Argentina. Shackleton was very angry. He roared at Blackbarrow, saying that all the men got very hungry on these expeditions and that he, the stowaway, would be the first to be eaten! Blackbarrow simply replied, 'They'd get a lot more meat off you, sir!' Shackleton couldn't help laughing and he ended up letting the young man join the party. Blackbarrow became a valued member of the team but was later to develop severe frostbite (see page 56).

Trapped and crushed

On 18 January 1915, *Endurance*, with twenty-eight men on board, got trapped in solid pack-ice in the Weddell Sea. Unluckily for them the ice had come early that year. She drifted north-west in a cold frozen world for nine months. The men hunted seals and penguins for food. It was a long, boring time to be stuck on a ship and the men did the best they could to entertain themselves. They played various games along the way and discovered that their 'boss', Shackleton, was an expert at 'Animal, Vegetable or Mineral'!

Then pressure ridges started to form on the ice and close in on the ship. She was now in danger of being completely crushed. On 27 October 1915 Shackleton ordered the men off the ship to camp on the ice. They called this place Ocean Camp. About a month later, the men watched in horror as the ice finally closed in on the ship and the poor *Endurance* was crushed to pieces:

Two massive floes, miles of ice, jammed her sides and held her fast, while the third floe tore across her stern, ripping off the rudder as though it had been made of match wood. She quivered and groaned as rudder and stern-post were torn off, and part of her keel was driven upwards by the ice. The shock of the impact was indescribable. To us it was as though the whole world were in the throes of an earthquake.

Frank Worsley, Captain of the *Endurance*

The huskies watch as the *Endurance* sinks, crushed by the ice. Photographer Frank Hurley managed to take this famous photograph.

With the ship gone, so were their chances of crossing the Antarctic – and of getting home. What were they going to do now? The men first tried to haul the supplies they had rescued from the ship over the ice to islands they knew were 500 km away, but the enormous ice ridges they came across meant they could only travel about 2 km a day. Exhausted, they stopped to set up a second camp on a large ice-floe. They called it Patience Camp. Shackleton kept them busy and fit with a daily routine, organizing hunts for seals and penguins, and even football matches! They drifted along until, on 8 April 1916, another crisis happened. The ice-floe began to split up:

The watchman raised the alarm that the floe was splintering. Our camp was reduced to an overcrowded rocking triangle, and it was evident that we must take the first opportunity to escape, no matter how desperate the chances might be.
Frank Hurley, expedition photographer

Shackleton and his men drag the James Caird *lifeboat across the ice after being stranded on the ice-floes. This boat would later save their lives.*

The men set off in the three lifeboats they had taken from the *Endurance*. It was a difficult journey, battling through the floes. At night, they made camp on a large ice-floe. However, Shackleton suddenly awoke with a bad feeling. It was lucky he did, as an enormous crack then appeared in the floe and Shackleton got there just in time to pull out one of his men from the water, who had fallen through the crack in his sleeping bag. Seconds later, the crack closed up!

They battled for a week through the sea until they reached Elephant Island, in the South Shetland Islands – the first land they had set foot on for twenty months. The men were shattered and exhausted. Shackleton himself had not slept for 100 hours. They were still a long way from real safety, though. Yes, they had reached land, but the problem was that no one knew they were there, so there was no chance of rescue. Shackleton decided he had to go with a small team to look for help.

At 61°S, Elephant Island is a small, bleak uninhabited place. It's only 38 km long and 19 km at its widest. The island got its name in the 1820s when elephant seals were hunted there. Shackleton's men were able to eat these seals as well as the island's penguins.

But where could he look? Well, he decided to make for the island of South Georgia, where there was a whaling station. Sounds easy enough, but there were a few problems:

• The island was over 1,300 km away.
• It meant travelling across one of the world's stormiest, most dangerous oceans.
• The men only had a choice of three small boats.

In any other circumstances this trip would have been an insane idea. Even if the men didn't get killed on the voyage, they could easily miss South Georgia itself. The odds were totally against them succeeding, but Shackleton decided they had to try. It was their only hope.

The journey of the *James Caird*

The men decided to make their voyage in the *James Caird*, a seven-metre lifeboat. They made the boat as seaworthy as they could, using pieces from the other two boats. A sledge and some packing-case lids were used as a framework for a deck, which was covered in canvas. The heavy seas could break the small boat's back so a mast from another boat was laid inside her as reinforcement. Shackleton selected five men to go with him.

The journey in the *James Caird* was to be one of the most heroic ones anyone has ever taken. It took them sixteen days. They faced fierce gales and enormous waves, including one that completely swamped their boat. The men were soaked through and freezing cold throughout. Their arms and legs became numb and swollen.

Shackleton tried to get a routine established which would help keep the men going:

Our meals were regular ... this point was essential, since the conditions of the voyage made increasing calls upon our vitality. Breakfast, at 8 a.m., consisted of a pannikin of hot hoosh made from Bovril sledging ration, two biscuits and some lumps of sugar. Lunch came at 1 p.m. and comprised Bovril sledging ration, eaten raw, and a pannikin of hot milk for each man. Tea, at 5 p.m., had the same menu ... The meals were the bright beacons in those cold and stormy days. The glow of warmth and comfort produced by the food and drink made optimists of us all.
Shackleton, *South*, 1919

Worsley (Captain of the *Endurance*), whose amazing navigational skills actually got them to South Georgia, wrote how Shackleton kept a constant eye on the state of the men:

He seemed to keep a mental finger on each man's pulse. If he noted one with signs of the strain telling on him, he would order hot milk and soon all would be swallowing the scalding, life-giving drink to the especial benefit of the man, all unaware, for whom it had been ordered.

Yet, even with Shackleton as their leader, the men began to become tired and weak. They were unable to get any proper rest in the horrendous conditions they were enduring. The waves rose up like solid walls of water threatening to swamp their little boat and the roaring noise of the wind and sea rang in their ears. Days ran into nights as the men worked round the clock, steering, working the sails, pumping out water and trying to eat and sleep in between. Then they ran out of water and became so thirsty that their tongues swelled up and they could not even eat.

THE ENDURANCE EXPEDITION

South Georgia
(Whaling station on south side)

Endurance enters pack-ice
11 Dec 1914

16-day route of James Caird lifeboat

Elephant Island
(men left here)

By boat to Elephant Island

Endurance sinks
21 Nov 1915

Shackleton and men leave trapped ship
27 Oct 1915

WEDDELL SEA

ANTARCTIC PENINSULA

Ice drift

RONNE ICE SHELF

Ship gets stuck in ice
19 Jan 1915

Land ahoy!

After 16 days of fighting the stormy seas, finally the island of South Georgia came into view! Yet their ordeal was not over. Instead of landing on the north coast (at the whaling station), they were forced to try and land on the south coast. This was probably the most dangerous part of the voyage. As they tried to land, gigantic waves struck them with the force of a stone wall. Water squirted into the boat through every seam and crack. For three hours the crew thought they were looking into the jaws of death as they came close to being wrecked. In his writings, Worsley says he found himself getting furious, because if they had perished then no one would ever have known how far they had come!

Eventually the men did manage to land on a small beach, shattered, but safe. Or were they? The terrible journey was not over yet. This part of the island was totally uninhabited. This meant they still had to cross the island to get to the whaling station on the north coast. After falling down on their knees to drink from a stream, their first water in days, they had to keep going.

Climbing for their lives

And so, after that arduous boat journey, Shackleton took the fittest two men, Worsley and Crean, with him, to climb over an unexplored mountain range with glaciers and steep precipices (a bit like climbing in parts of the European Alps). Each man took food for three days in a boot tied round their neck. They also had a stove for cooking, a box of matches, a lamp, a rope, an axe to make footholes in any ice they might have to climb, and the log book of all their journeys. They were so exhausted they did not dare go to sleep in case they never woke up again. Fortunately Shackleton's luck held out and they had good weather and a full moon during the night to light their way.

This journey would have been difficult even for an experienced mountaineer. Shackleton and his men did not have any proper equipment for climbing, or skis to help them cross the snow. At every step they sank up to their knees, their boots slipping and sliding in the snow. They had to cross steep ice ridges, slowly cutting steps into the ice with their axe in parts. At one point the men came to a 500-metre ice slope. Would they really have to cut steps into it all the way down? Luckily, Shackleton had a better idea – they would toboggan all the way down, sitting on coiled-up pieces of rope! This they did and it proved an exhilarating ride!

When they had crossed the mountains they were still not certain of safety. First of all they had to guess which was the right valley to descend into. They made a calculated choice and, 36 hours after leaving the south coast, they heard the siren of the whaling station. What a relief that must have been! Apparently the first three men who saw them fled from their wild appearance! They had long beards, tangled hair, tattered clothes and no doubt smelt horrible!

Shackleton walked towards the Norwegian station manager. It was Saturday 20 May 1916. He recorded their first conversation:

'My name is Shackleton,' I said.
Immediately he put out his hand and said, 'Come in. Come in.'
'Tell me, when was the war over?' I asked.
'The war is not over,' he answered. 'Millions are being killed. Europe is mad. The world is mad.'

> The *James Caird* boat is usually displayed in Shackleton's old school: Dulwich College, London. It can sometimes be seen in exhibitions around the world.

Return to Elephant Island

Shackleton tried several times, with different ships, to reach the men left behind on Elephant Island. Finally, at the end of August he managed to get back on a small Chilean steamer. And all 22 men were still alive! Shackleton counted them nervously through his binoculars as he approached the island. Was he relieved! The men had been there for 105 days. They had made huts out of the remaining two lifeboats. Apparently one of the things they had dreamed of during their long wait had been suet pudding!

And the rest of the men?

Let's not forget the men who had arrived on the Ross Sea side of the Antarctic at the beginning of the expedition in order to lay the supplies for Shackleton's crossing.

This group *had* landed at Cape Evans in January 1915 as planned. They had moored their ship, *Aurora*, to the ice for the winter, but then disaster had struck. They had only unloaded a few of the supplies when the *Aurora* got blown away in a very bad blizzard in May, along with the rest of the crew and much of the stores and food.

The men left on the shore managed to survive for two winters. They found some food and equipment left from previous expeditions and caught seals for meat and blubber. Despite all their own hardships they didn't touch the supplies which were intended for Shackleton's polar-crossing party and still managed to lay all the depots! They obviously had no idea that the expedition had been abandoned.

They also had the worry, like those on Elephant Island, that no one might ever find them. Only the *Aurora*'s crew knew their exact position, and now they were missing, presumed dead.

However, unknown to them, the *Aurora* had survived. After being blown away by the blizzard she had been trapped in the pack-ice for ten months. Eventually the ice melted and she got to New Zealand. From there she set out to rescue the men at Cape Evans. Shackleton was now on board, having rescued all his men from the Weddell Sea side. The Cape Evans survivors were astounded to see Shackleton arrive by sea, rather than from over the ice behind them! Three men had died in the Ross Sea party, but a survivor, Dick Richards (who lived to be 90), said that, although he had never recovered from the experience, 'It was something that the human spirit had accomplished.'

The final journey
In 1922 Shackleton set off for Antarctica again, with the aim of mapping 3,000 km of its coastline. He died on board his ship, *Quest,* of a heart attack and was buried on South Georgia Island, according to his wife's wishes.

Extreme expeditions and leadership skills
Shackleton's leadership skills are now being studied by American businesses! They are using extracts from his diaries and those of his men to give lessons in management, leadership and communication. They see him as an example of someone who in a crisis will stand up and take responsibility, someone who is a good example for modern managers.

Why was Shackleton such a good leader? Well, he always kept his men informed and asked for their opinions and ideas. He was thorough and planned for all possibilities, but he was always prepared to start from scratch if something went wrong. His optimism, stamina and patience inspired his men, and he managed them well.

An example of this is shown when one of Shackleton's men became suicidal after the expedition landed on Elephant Island. They had just suffered five days of terrifying gales in a tiny lifeboat. Shackleton decided to put him in charge of cooking. With something important to occupy his mind the man began to think of other things rather than of his own miseries.

Shackleton wrote:

The task of keeping the galley fire alight took his thoughts away from the chances of immediate dissolution. In fact, I found him a little later gravely concerned over the drying of a naturally not over-clean pair of socks, hung up close to our evening milk.

Freezing photography

The photographer on Shackleton's *Endurance* expedition was an Australian called Frank Hurley. He went back to the sinking *Endurance* to save 150 of his best negatives, which is why we have the photographs of this expedition as a record of the trip (see pages 107 and 108). On Scott's last expedition the photographer had been an Englishman called Herbert Ponting. Both men took excellent photographs in extreme conditions. Even photography with modern equipment is difficult in polar regions because the cold slows up batteries if the temperature drops to −10°C or less. To protect your fingers and face against cold burn it is best to cover the exposed metal parts of the camera with insulating tape or something similar.

The Shackleton film

Always a professional, Hurley filmed the last moments of the *Endurance* as it was crushed by the ice and sank. Hurley kept the film safe throughout the following long months in the Antarctic. The result, *South*, was first shown by Shackleton in 1919. The film has recently been restored and shows some amazing footage of the sinking ship and its crew – look out for a showing of it near you!

EXTREME
EXPLORATION TODAY

Since the so-called 'heroic age' of Scott and Shackleton there have been many more expeditions to both the North and South Poles, right up to the present day. Men and women of all nationalities still struggle against the extreme conditions in the Arctic and Antarctic. Though we now have modern equipment and technology to help, these expeditions can still be very dangerous because the polar regions are such wild, unpredictable areas of the world. Even if someone is in radio contact, atmospheric conditions mean that the radio may not work. White-outs, blizzards and other extreme weather conditions mean that immediate rescue by a plane may not be possible if something goes wrong. The best thing to do is to try to be prepared as much as possible for the unexpected. Remember that in the Arctic, you could meet an unfriendly polar bear or fall through the ice into the sea. In the Antarctic there is the threat of crevasses, plus the problems of mountains, not to mention the icy katabatic winds.

Modern polar explorers are always amazed by how much the early explorers achieved with so little knowledge and no sophisticated equipment. They have great admiration for them!

TRANS-ANTARCTICA — UNSUPPORTED

One expedition really caught the imagination of the public at the end of the twentieth century. It summed up the excitement, terror and difficulties of venturing out into the polar regions, even today. This was the two-man British manhauling expedition undertaken by Sir Ranulph Fiennes and Dr Mike Stroud. They set out to cross the Antarctic continent via the South Pole on 9 November 1992 without any support at all. This meant they pulled all their own food and supplies on sledges behind them. Their sledges were an enormous weight – almost 230 kg each at the start; like tugging nearly 100 bricks! They had no airdrops, no supply depots, no motorized transport, just their own strength and perseverance.

They crossed from the Weddell Sea to the Ross Ice Shelf. During the ninety-five days of their journey, they fell down crevasses, suffered frostbite, got hypothermia, became severely depressed and nearly starved to death! Despite walking for 2,000 km, they did not quite get to the very edge of the Ross Ice Shelf as they had hoped to do. Even so, their achievement in successfully crossing the Antarctic landmass was extraordinary and has yet to be beaten.

EXTREME FACTS
HYPOTHERMIA

Hypothermia happens when the body loses heat faster than it can produce it. Someone can go from very cold to dangerously cold very quickly, often because of a mixture of wind, wet clothes, tiredness and hunger.

Symptoms?

Exhaustion, numb skin (especially fingers and toes), stumbling around, slurred speech, dizziness, muscle cramps and irrational behaviour (i.e. sufferers saying they are warm and trying to take their clothes off in freezing temperatures).

What can you do about it?
Treat hypothermia by getting the patient out of the wind. Remove any wet clothing as quickly as possible and replace it with warm, dry clothing. Next, give the sufferer some hot liquids (but not alcohol) and some high-calorie food that can be easily digested. The human body functions normally at 37°C and hypothermia sets in when the temperature falls below 35°C. Below 32°C the victim just wants to go to sleep, which can be fatal.

In true polar tradition, Fiennes and Stroud were carrying out scientific research on their expedition. As a doctor, Mike Stroud wanted to look at nutrition, human fitness and the control of body weight. The men kept regular urine samples. One night they were so bored in their tent, they used the filled sample bottles for playing chess on a large board they had drawn on a wooden box!

WORKING IN THE EXTREMES
Many people today go to work in the Arctic and Antarctic. They are very often scientists looking at everything from geology to the polar environment. In the Arctic they often have links with towns and airstrips around the edge of the Arctic Circle (i.e. in northern Canada), but on the Antarctic continent their bases have to be totally self-sufficient. Food and other supplies have to be flown in and, during the terrible weather of the dark polar winter months, there can be no deliveries. Those who stay during the winter in one of the various permanent stations here might have more comfortable living conditions

than the early explorers, but they can still suffer from the problems of continual darkness and depression.

There are also the basic problems of everyday life to deal with, such as:

- Keeping warm
- Food and shelter
- Going to the toilet
- Washing yourself and your clothes

In the main bases in Antarctica there are good cooking facilities, heating, showers, washing-machines and proper toilets (or at least Portaloos). However, life in the field camps and on field trips can be slightly different. A field camp is a temporary camp built for carrying out research in the surrounding area.

EXTREME FACTS
TOILET TRIPS IN ANTARCTICA!

In field camps on the ice, the quality of the 'toilets' can vary considerably. Journalist Sara Wheeler spent seven months living on the continent of Antarctica and described some of the possibilities:

1) Cut a hole in the sea ice (with windbreakers round it), but watch out in case it has frozen over if you go to the toilet at night! Also beware of seals popping up for air through the hole while you are relieving yourself!

2) Mark a spot with a 'pee flag' so the staining of the ice only

happens in one place. Easy for men to go here but not so convenient for women, since they are mostly in full view of the camp and have to pull their clothes down, exposing a bare bottom! This is because clothing such as long johns is usually designed for men.

3) If you are lucky, you'll be in a large camp that has a special toilet hut. However, the fun comes later. There is usually a system of bagging up the toilet's frozen contents to take back to the base for disposal (do you think there are many volunteers for that job?).

4) Sometimes liquid human waste, as well as solid, is flown out. This is from areas such as the Dry Valleys (on the edge of the Antarctic continent) where scientists study nitrates in the soil and in the frozen lakes. Any human waste would spoil their research. Here everyone is obliged to carry a pee bottle with them which is later emptied into a barrel – very organized! Girls and women take note: pee bottles are designed for men, though some women do use them when there is little alternative.

The problems of going to the toilet in the freezing cold are described by Dr Mike Stroud:

'When it was cold, as long as you bared all quickly and settled with cheeks to the wind, it was not the private parts that were the limiting factor but the hands which got too cold. When it came to the job of clearing up, one could just not use toilet paper with mitts on. However, whatever the wind and weather had to offer, we generally coped with this essential everyday activity in good humour.'

'Bothie'

The only dog that has been recorded as peeing at both the North and South Poles is Sir Ranulph Fiennes' Jack Russell terrier, Bothie. Bothie flew in with Fiennes' wife, Ginnie, to meet the Transglobe Expedition (1979–82) at each Pole.

Keeping clean?

If you are not too keen on a daily bath or shower, a field camp in the Antarctic is the place to be! Here it's far too cold to want to keep washing. People out on camps often don't wash at all. There are some good reasons why:

• Nothing really smells here because it is too cold
• Collecting the water to do the washing is a major effort in itself

Wetwipes and babywipes are used, but they tend to freeze up and so have to be kept in your sleeping bag – along with everything else that needs to be kept warm, like water bottles, batteries and dry clothes for morning!

People hauling their sledges across the continent do have to force themselves to wash every so often, or at least to roll in the snow like a horse, to avoid painful sores from the harnesses they wear.

And what about washing clothes?

There's not a lot of this on field camps either. Instead underpants may be turned inside out, or a pair just worn until the ones taken off last week seem clean by comparison!

SOME POLAR PROBLEMS

An extract from a geologist's field camp notebook entitled 'It's Cold!'

1) Anything in a tube is frozen, e.g. toothpaste, sun cream, lipsalve. (If you want to use it in the morning put it in your sleeping bag with you!)

2) All food is frozen, or near frozen, i.e. jam and peanut butter are almost frozen, cans of fruit and vegetables are frozen, energy bars are brittle, not chewy.

3) Materials such as nylon are more brittle and develop crinkles.

4) Nose dribble 'snot' freezes on contact with sunglasses, gloves and anoraks – though the good thing is it can be brushed off as a solid.

5) Urine (wee) either blows away before hitting the ground or freezes instantly on contact with rocks.

6) Faeces (solid human waste) freeze rapidly, making waste disposal easier.

7) Clean wipes freeze in their box.

Allan Ashworth, geologist, 6 December 1995, latitude 85°S (about 500 km from the South Pole)

Food on field camps

A combination of cold and hard work makes people very hungry and they will need a lot more energy than normal. An average person will burn up something like 2,000–2,500 calories a day, but in extreme cold this increases.

Calorie count

- Someone manhauling their own sledge needs 7,000–10,000 calories a day.
- Someone with a dog sledge needs up to 5,000 calories a day.
- Travelling on a Skidoo (a motorized sledge) needs about 3,350 calories a day.
- Working inside a research station requires only about 2,750 calories a day.

Even with today's Skidoos, food rations must be light and compact for people working at remote field camps so they can be transported easily. They also need to be quick and easy to prepare to save the limited supply of fuel (which also needs to be carried with them).

The food is packed into 'per day' rations. It must contain both energy to keep the body active and a range of nutrients to keep the body healthy. British Antarctic Survey field rations consist mainly of freeze-dried meat, several varieties of dried soup, dried vegetables, rice, tea, coffee, drinking chocolate, orange drink, biscuits, chocolate, butter, sugar, dried milk and multi-vitamin pills. Water is produced by melting snow. Paraffin-fired Primus stoves are still used because they are dependable and durable.

In the polar regions it is possible to get dehydrated very quickly because the air is so dry. This makes sweat evaporate very quickly and so a lot of fluid is lost from the body. Explorers need to keep drinking.

MODERN POLAR CLOTHES

Modern explorers and people working in the Arctic and Antarctic still follow the native people's principle of wearing several layers.

Hands and feet

It is better to wear mittens rather than gloves, as fingers stay warmer when they are touching each other. Your feet sweat more than any other part of your body so they are more likely to get frostbitten. Special boots must be worn when working outside (see diagram on facing page).

Layer 1: Underwear

Long-sleeved thermal vest

Thermal mitten liners

Long johns

Underwear should not be made of cotton as this can absorb water (sweat). Modern fabrics like polypropylene trap air and draw the moisture away, but keep in the body's heat.

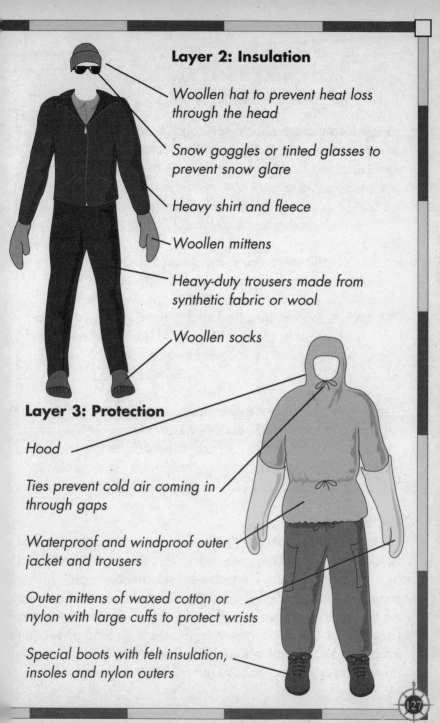

Layer 2: Insulation

Woollen hat to prevent heat loss through the head

Snow goggles or tinted glasses to prevent snow glare

Heavy shirt and fleece

Woollen mittens

Heavy-duty trousers made from synthetic fabric or wool

Woollen socks

Layer 3: Protection

Hood

Ties prevent cold air coming in through gaps

Waterproof and windproof outer jacket and trousers

Outer mittens of waxed cotton or nylon with large cuffs to protect wrists

Special boots with felt insulation, insoles and nylon outers

EXTREME FACTS
COLD BURN

It is possible to get a burn from touching something extremely cold, just as you get burned from touching something very hot. Anything made from metal that is exposed to a very low temperature (batteries or a camera, for example) can give you a nasty cold burn. It is even possible for your skin to become frozen to the surface of the object.

On the *Discovery* expedition (page 25) one of the men opened a jar of jam, put some on a knife and then into his mouth. The knife was so cold that it immediately froze fast to his lips and tongue. If he had tried to remove it, it would have torn his skin away. He had to wait and get the knife warmed up before it could be taken away.

Tips

Don't wear metal-framed spectacles, earrings or rings in polar conditions because you are more likely to get cold burn and frostbite! If you have to take your gloves off for any reason, you should always keep wearing the glove-liners for protection.

Tents

For the last 100 years most polar explorers have used pyramid tents and this is still the case today. This design can withstand high winds and flying ice particles and is easy to put up in a storm. The door is often shaped like a funnel and about a metre off the ground. Nowadays these tents are designed for two people. For insulation, there is a built-in ground sheet, an inflatable airbed and a sheepskin. The sleeping bags have a down-filled outer bag and a synthetic pile inner bag.

The manhauling team of Fiennes and Stroud preferred to use a dome-shaped tent because it was lighter to carry on their sledges but they found that it was difficult to put up in strong winds and its poles could easily get bent.

Improvements

Polar experts are always experimenting to improve their equipment, especially clothing, rations and shelters. Living, working and travelling conditions have improved greatly from the times of the early explorers. But we must remember that it was often these men's mistakes (and sometimes their deaths) which led to the realization that certain changes were needed. Nowadays the development of man-made materials and more ways of processing and packing food provide constant opportunities for experimentation.

AN EXPLORER'S 'SHOPPING LIST'

If you are exploring the polar regions, you will need to take lots of equipment, but you must try to keep the weight down as much as possible. This is especially important if you are man-hauling your own load. After just a few hours carrying a ruck-sack and pulling a heavy load in the freezing cold, you will have used up a lot of energy and will feel very tired.

Special food is manufactured for explorers, which can be in dehydrated form so that it is very light and easy to carry. You then add hot water (melt down ice and snow on your cooker) to the food to make it into a healthy meal.

Here are just a few of the items you might find on a polar explorer's 'shopping list':

Tent (specially designed for polar use)

Small cooker with spare parts

Mugs, plates, pans, etc.

Fuel, such as paraffin

Sleeping bags – outer and inner

Rope

Ice axe and snow shovel

Pee bottle

Toilet paper

Emergency beacon/flares (in case you get into trouble and need to be rescued)

Batteries – lots (watch out for cold burn when touching them)

Radio, camera, video camera

Food bags – with calories and daily rations measured out in advance

Skis and snow shoes

Snow goggles (to prevent snow glare)

Specialist clothes, hooded windproof jacket, mittens, etc.

Tools, such as spanner, screws, etc. (if something essential like the cooker breaks down you must be able to repair it)

Smaller items

Maps and compass

Swiss army knife (has lots of different attachments so very useful for all sorts of tasks)

Diary and pens/pencils (to record what you've seen and done)

Lip balm and hand cream (skin on lips and hands will be cracked and blistered from the cold)

Needle and thread (for repairs to clothes/tent)

Waterproof and windproof matches

First-aid kit: medicines, antiseptic cream, plasters, etc.

WHAT'S IN STORE FOR THE POLAR LANDS?

ARE THERE ANY EXTREME RECORDS LEFT TO BREAK?

Even now, many people see it as a great achievement to reach either the North or South Pole. However, extreme explorers usually want to break records. Extreme expeditions are made either to places that no one has been to before or in a way that no one has ever done before. Even today, any expedition to the Arctic or Antarctic involves risk and danger because of the forces of nature. But what actual records remain to be broken in the polar regions? Well, Sir Ranulph Fiennes and Mike Stroud broke records by pulling their own sledges right across the Antarctic continent, while David Hempleman-Adams included the Poles in what he calls 'an explorer's Grand Slam', by reaching both the North and South Geographic and Magnetic Poles, and by climbing the highest mountain in each of the seven continents (including Everest). Can you think of a record that would make *you* an extreme explorer to the polar regions?

THE POLES AND THE ENVIRONMENT

Both the Arctic and Antarctic are being affected by world environmental problems, such as pollution and global warming. Some of the world's top scientists think that global warming could cause huge changes in the polar regions. Remember, 70 per cent of the world's fresh water is in the Antarctic ice-cap alone.

One theory suggests that if ice shelves in Antarctica melt faster than at the present, the sea level of the entire world could rise. This would mean that many of the low-lying parts of the world – like the Polynesian island states – could vanish under water. A theory also suggests that at some stage in the future it may not be possible to reach the North Pole over the sea ice because global warming seems to be melting more and more of it each year. Scientists are constantly monitoring developments. It was scientists working at a British Antarctic research station who first identified a hole in the earth's ozone layer in 1981. The ozone layer protects the earth from many of the harmful effects of the sun's rays. Samples taken by scientists from the ice in the Arctic and Antarctic show how pollution from world industrial development has spread to even these remote areas.

THE ANTARCTIC TREATY

No country or person or group owns Antarctica. Seven countries claim a sector of the continent: Britain, New Zealand, Norway, Chile, Argentina, Australia and France (with some claims overlapping). Under an agreement known as the Antarctic Treaty, the continent is seen as a world scientific resource.

The treaty states that 'Antarctica shall be used for peaceful measures only … in the interests of all humanity'. The original treaty was signed by 12 nations in 1959 and by 1996 this had reached 43. Any country can join but to have an official say in consultations the nation must maintain a scientific involvement in the continent, which really means a research base. By 1997 there were about 35 permanently manned stations, about 25 summer-only bases, and about 200 summer scientific huts on the continent. In the summer there are about 5,000 scientists and support staff living there. Only about 1,000 people remain during the dark winter months.

In 1991 the Antarctic Treaty nations said that huskies were not natural to the Antarctic environment and so should be no longer allowed there. There is now a sledge monument to the husky dogs of the past. They were no longer really needed anyway because motorized vehicles that can work reliably in Antarctic conditions have now been developed, such as Skidoos and Snocats.

THE ARCTIC

Unlike the Antarctic, eight countries – Canada, Greenland, Norway, Sweden, Finland, Russia, USA (Alaska), Iceland – actually have land inside the Arctic Circle. Alaska and Canada have begun to give back some lands and rights to the native Arctic peoples, though this is often in exchange for being allowed to extract minerals in the area. In 1990 the International Arctic Science Committee (IASC) was formed to co-ordinate scientific research in the region.

WOMEN AT THE POLES

Early expeditions to the polar regions were always all-male and often based on a naval way of life. Women were left out because of the attitudes of the time. People didn't think of women as explorers or adventurers and would not have believed that they could cope with the harsh physical conditions. There was also a lack of privacy for them. It was not until 1935 that the first woman set foot on the Antarctic continent – Norwegian Caroline

Mikkelsen, the wife of a whaling captain.

These days, women often go on expeditions to both the North and South Poles. They also work on scientific research in both the Arctic and Antarctic. However, there are many more men than women to be found travelling and working in these areas.

TOURISM IN THE POLAR REGIONS

It's incredible to think that the places where so many extreme expeditions took place are now becoming tourist areas. For example there is a museum in the frozen north of Canada showing the suffering that Franklin and his crew went through on their tragic expedition. And, in Antarctica, tourism is a growing industry (though not many people go there on holiday yet – it's very expensive). Ships take people on tours to view the landscape and wildlife, as well as giving them the opportunity to step on to the Antarctic continent, something that very few can say they have done.

The Antarctic Treaty has drawn up a set of rules for these visitors. The most important is:

Don't take anything away and don't leave anything behind.

And finally ...

There are many, many more stories about extreme expeditions in the polar regions, both early and modern. All these journeys have been difficult and full of adventures, but unfortunately it's been impossible to write about them all in this book. Some are mentioned in the Timeline (see page 135), so you may want to find out more about them for yourself. And, if you ever set off to either of the Poles yourself, watch out for the dangers mentioned in this book, and good luck — something which all explorers need!

POLAR TIMELINE

The nationalities of these explorers are given, but remember that their teams were often made up of a mixture of people from different countries and were sometimes funded by other countries.

THE ARCTIC

BC

330   Pytheas (Phoenician) may have reached Iceland.

AD

c.500   Irish monks sail to Iceland.

860   Vikings reach Iceland.

982–5   Erik the Red lands on Greenland with Norwegian settlers.

c.1400   England trades with Iceland.

1524   Verrazano (Italian) reaches Hudson Bay.

1535   Cartier (French) sails to Montreal.

1553   English merchants send ships to look for the North-east Passage.

1576–8   Frobisher (British) makes three voyages to search for the North-west Passage.

1585–7   Davis (British) makes three voyages to search for the North-west Passage.

1594–7   Barents (Dutch) makes three voyages to search for the North-east Passage and spends the winter at 76°N.

1609–11	Hudson (British) makes two trips to look for the North-east Passage. He disappears in Hudson Bay.
1725–42	Bering (Danish) leads two Russian expeditions to explore the north coast of Siberia and the Bering Strait.
1818	John Ross (British) searches for the North-west Passage.
1819–20	Parry (British) wins a prize of £5,000 for being the first European to reach 110°W. Overwinters off Melville Island.
1831	James Clark Ross (British) discovers the Magnetic North Pole.
1845–7	Franklin (British) searches for the North-west Passage and loses his life in the attempt.
1847–57	Many expeditions look for Franklin and his crew.
1879–81	The *Jeannette* (US) expedition is crushed by ice in the Arctic Ocean.
1895	Nansen (Norwegian) drifts aboard *Fram* and then sledges to 86°N.
1903–5	Amundsen (Norwegian) sails the North-west Passage on the *Gjøa*.
1908	April, date that Cook (US) claims to have reached the North Pole.
1909	April, date that Peary (US) claims to have reached the North Pole.
1926	May, Amundsen passes over the North Pole in an airship with Ellsworth (Norwegian/US/Italian expedition). In the same month Byrd (US) claims to have flown over North Pole in a plane.

1935   International expedition climbs highest peak – Gunnbjørnsfjaeld, Greenland, 3,693 m.

1948   Gordiyenko (Soviet) lands at the North Pole in a plane.

1958   US nuclear-powered submarine USS *Nautilius* crosses under the North Pole. A record exists of the sounds of the journey.

1959   US submarine *Skate* surfaces at the North Pole itself.

1968   Plaisted (US) and three others reach the North Pole over the ice, using snow-scooters and being supplied by plane drops.

1969   Wally Herbert (British) and three companions make first crossing of the Arctic Ocean with dog sledges. Three air-drops.

1977   Soviet ice breaker *Arktika* reaches the North Pole through the ice (taking the first woman to North Pole).

1978   Uemura (Japanese) makes the first solo journey to the North Pole with one sledge and 17 dogs (he flies back after he has reached it).

1979   Shparo (Soviet) and six companions reach the North Pole after a march of 1,500 km without dogs or sledges.

1982   Fiennes and Burton (British) become first men to reach both Poles overland (as part of Transglobe Expedition which circumnavigates the globe via the Poles).

THE ANTARCTIC

AD

c.650   Ui-te-Rangiora (Polynesian) sails south until he reaches a frozen sea.

1497	Vasco da Gama (Portuguese) sails round Cape of Good Hope (South Africa), showing it is not connected to a southern continent.
1520	Magellan (Portuguese leading a Spanish expedition) sails round South America.
1642	Tasman (Dutch) discovers Tasmania and the west coast of New Zealand.
1772–5	Cook (British) sails across the Antarctic Circle but does not sight the continent.
1820	Bellinghausen (Estonian leading a Russian expedition) is probably the first person to see the Antarctic continent.
1822–4	Weddell (British) reaches 74°15′, the Weddell Sea.
1837–40	D'Urville (French) circumnavigates Antarctica and names part of the continent after his wife, Adélie.
1838–42	Six-ship, US expedition led by Wilkes circumnavigates the continent the opposite way to D'Urville.
1839–43	James Clark Ross (British) discovers Ross Ice Shelf.
1897–9	Crew of *Belgica* (Belgian) winter, unintentionally, in pack-ice.
1898–1900	First expedition to spend winter on the continent, led by Borchgrevink (Norwegian leading a British expedition).
1901–4	Scott's (British) first expedition. Attempt on South Pole, reaches 82°S.
1907–9	Shackleton's (British) *Nimrod* expedition reaches 88°S. Mawson (Australian) reaches the Magnetic South Pole.

1910–12	Amundsen's Antarctic Expedition. December 1911, reaches South Pole.
1910–13	Scott's second expedition. January 1912, reaches Pole. March 1912, Scott and companions die on return.
1911–14	Australian Antarctic Expedition. December 1912, Ninnis dies in crevasse. February 1913, Mawson struggles into base camp.
1914–16	Shackleton's *Endurance* expedition. Original aim is to cross Antarctica.
1929	Byrd (US) claims to have flown over South Pole in a plane.
1935	Ellsworth (US) flies across the Antarctic continent.
1956	US builds a scientific research station at the South Pole.
1955–8	Fuchs (British) crosses Antarctica with Snocats. Support party led by Hillary (NZ). Supplied by air.
1966	International expedition climbs the highest peak, Vinson Massif, 4,897 m.
1968–9	Japanese expedition travels to the South Pole and back.
1969	12 November, first women (NZ/US) reach the South Pole. Arrive by plane and the five link arms to reach the Pole together.
1980–1	Fiennes, Burton and Shepard (British) cross continent with snow-mobiles as part of Transglobe Expedition.
1989–90	Steger (US) leads international expedition for the first crossing of Antarctica on foot, with dog sledges.
1992–3	Fiennes and Stroud (British) manhaul sledges across the whole continent, the first humans to do so.

GLOSSARY

Altitude
The height of something in relation to the ground. At high altitudes, in places like mountain tops, it can be difficult to breathe properly. This is because there is less oxygen the higher up you go. This may cause an illness called altitude sickness.

Base camp
A camp from which expeditions set out.

Bay
A place where the land curves inwards from the sea.

Blizzard
A very severe snowstorm with strong winds.

Blubber
The fat of sea mammals, such as seals and whales.

Cairn
A mound of stones built as a landmark or memorial.

Calorie
A unit of heat energy. It is usually used to measure the energy contained in food.

Cold burn
A burn caused by touching something which is extremely cold (often metal objects).

Crevasse
A deep, open crack, often found in glaciers.

Dehydration
This occurs when a person loses a lot of water from their body. Food can be dehydrated in order to preserve it and make it easier to carry.

Disorientated
A person is disorientated when they have become confused and have lost their sense of direction.

Dissect
To cut up a body, part or plant in order to study its internal parts.

Drift (ocean)
A current of water that can carry ships and other objects along with it.

'En Route'
A French phrase meaning 'during a journey or trip'.

Eskimo
General name originally given by the Europeans to the native peoples of northern Canada, Alaska, Greenland and eastern Siberia. Nowadays the peoples of north-west Canada and western Greenland prefer to be called Inuit (see **Inuit**).

Frostbite
A condition common in very cold climates, when body tissue becomes frozen. Can result in gangrene (see below).

Gangrene
The death of body tissue which can result from conditions such as frostbite. The affected area or limb may need to be removed (amputated).

Glacier
A mass of snow and ice which moves slowly under its own weight.

Hoosh
A kind of soup made from hot water and pemmican (see **Pemmican**).

Hummock
A mound, hump or ridge in an ice field.

Husky (dog)
A working dog that is used by the native peoples in the Arctic. They were also used on expeditions to the Antarctic in the past.

Hypothermia
A dangerous condition that happens when the body loses heat faster than it can produce it, when the body temperature falls below 35°C.

Iceberg
A very large chunk of floating ice that has broken off a glacier or ice shelf.

Icebreaker
A ship specially designed to cut through the ice.

Ice-floe
A piece of floating ice, smaller than an iceberg.

Ice shelf
An enormous area of ice that is permanently attached to the land.

Igloo
A dome-shaped house built from blocks of snow, from the Inuit word *iglu*, meaning house.

Insulation
A form of protection, using material that prevents the loss of heat.

Inuit
The name of the native people of north-west Canada and western Greenland (see **Eskimo**).

Katabatic winds
Strong, down-flowing winds that blow in the Antarctic.

Kayak
A type of canoe used originally by the Inuit.

Knot
A unit of speed used for ships, aircraft and winds. Equivalent to one nautical mile per hour (see **nautical mile**).

Latitude (lines of)
Imaginary horizontal lines that are used on maps of the world to give distances north and south of the equator.

Longitude (lines of)
Imaginary vertical lines that are used on maps of the world to give distances east and west of the prime meridian.

Manhauling
When people pull the sledges themselves (rather than husky dogs).

Meteorite
A piece of rock (or metal) that falls from outer space to the earth.

Morale
The confidence and enthusiasm of a person or group of people at a particular time.

Musket
An old-fashioned gun that is fired from the shoulder.

Mutiny
A rebellion against authority; usually describes soldiers or sailors rising up against their officers.

Nautical mile
Used for measuring distances at sea; a nautical mile is equivalent to 1.852 km or 1.15 land miles.

Nomadic
The traditional way of life of people who travel from place to place to find land for their animals.

Pack-ice
Large ice-floes floating in the sea which move around and can get pushed together, trapping ships.

Pemmican
Dried beef and beef fat, moulded into blocks (see **Hoosh**).

Permafrost
Ground that never thaws and is always below freezing point. Usually found in polar regions.

Pike
An old-fashioned weapon that has a pointed iron head on a long wooden shaft.

Plateau
An area of high, level ground.

Prefabricated
Or 'prefab', a building whose parts have been made in advance so that it can be easily assembled later on.

Pressure ridges
Ridges in the ground formed when movements force areas of snow and ice to be pushed up against each other.

RGS
Stands for the Royal Geographical Society. This organization still exists today.

Scurvy
A disease caused by lack of vitamin C, very common in explorers of the past.

Sextant
An instrument used for measuring angles between distances, which is used to find locations.

Silk Route (or Road)
An ancient trade route linking central China with Europe. Established under the Romans in Europe, it was named after the silk brought to the West from the East.

Skidoo
A kind of motorized sledge. One type is called a Sno-Cat.

Snow-blindness
A very painful eye condition caused by the bright glare of the snow and ice.

Snow-bridge
Snow that crosses (and often covers and hides) a crevasse. It may be possible to cross the bridge, depending on its strength.

Sponsor
A person or organization who provides funds for a project or activity, often in return for advertising and publicity.

Strait
A narrow passage of water connecting two large areas of water or seas.

Supply depots
Supplies of food and fuel left in advance and marked by flags by teams before the main expedition begins.

Telegram
An old-fashioned way of sending messages over long distances. The message is transmitted on a wire and delivered in writing.

Tundra
Means 'treeless', describes the grassland in the Arctic which is free of snow in the Arctic summer.

Whaler
A ship specially built for hunting whales.

White-out
A kind of optical illusion that can occur in overcast polar regions when you can't tell the difference between the sky and the ground.

Wind chill
The cooling effect of wind blowing on a surface.

FURTHER EXPLORATION

If you'd like to find out more about any of the explorers and expeditions that you've read about in this book, there are lots of things you can do. Look out for special exhibitions on the Poles and find out what's on at local museums. You can also find more books on these subjects in the library and look up web sites about polar exploration. Here are some to start you off:

Places to visit:
Scott's ship RRS *Discovery* at Discovery Point, Dundee Heritage Trust, Dundee, Scotland
The Explorers' Galleries, National Maritime Museum, Greenwich, London
Polar Gallery, The Dynamic Earth, Edinburgh, Scotland
Scott Polar Research Institute Museum, Cambridge (afternoons only)
The Oates Museum, Selbourne, Hampshire

Websites to visit:
British Antarctic Survey – http://www.antarctica.ac.uk
Scott Polar Research Institute –http://www.spri.cam.ac.uk/kids/home.htm

Some books you might enjoy reading:
The Arctic and Antarctic, Dorling Kindersley Eyewitness Guide, London, 1995
Beattie, Owen, Geiger John, with Tannka, S., *Buried in Ice, The Mystery of a Lost Arctic Expedition*, Hodder & Stoughton, London, 1992.
Mason, Anthony, Peary and Amundsen, *Race to the Poles*, Evans Brothers Ltd, London, 1995
Philips Atlas of Exploration (in association with RGS), 1996
Rootes David, *Exploration into the Polar Regions,* Belitha Press in association with the RGS, 1994.

Original films of early Antarctic expeditions
These are sometimes shown at specialist cinemas, such as the National Film Theatre in London:
South, Hurley's record of Shackleton's 1914 expedition, recently restored.
90° South, Ponting's film from Scott's second expedition, filmed 1910–11.

Bibliography

Alexander, Caroline, *The Endurance*, Bloomsbury plc, London, 1998

Antarctica, Lonely Planet Publications, London, 1996

Antarctica Schools Pack, Foreign & Commonwealth Office in collaboration with the British Antarctic Survey, 1999

The Arctic and Antarctic, Dorling Kindersley Eyewitness Guide, London, 1995

Beattie, Owen, Geiger, John, with Tannka, S., *Buried in Ice, The Mystery of a Lost Arctic Expedition*, Hodder & Stoughton, London, 1992

Burch, S., *The Eskimos*, Macdonald Orbis, London, 1998

Cherry-Garrard, Apsley, *The Worst Journey in the World*, Picador 1994

Crosley, Louise, *Explore Antarctica*, Cambridge University Press, Cambridge, 1995

Curtis Neil, Allaby, Michael, *Planet Earth*, Kingfisher Books, New York, 1993

Discovery Point's Education Pack, Dundee Heritage Trust, Dundee (regularly updated).

The Dorling Kindersley Geography of the World, Dorling Kindersley, London, 1996

Fiennes, Ranulph, *Living Dangerously*, Macmillan, London, 1994

Fiennes, Ranulph, *Mind over Matter*, Mandarin, London, 1994

Harrowfield, David L., *Icy Heritage*, Antarctic Heritage Trust, 1995

Hempleman-Adams, David, *Walking on Thin Ice,* Orion, London, 1998

Hooper, Meredith, *A for Antarctica*, Piccolo, London, 1991

Huntford, Roland, *Shackleton*, Hodder and Stoughton, London, 1985

Huntford, Roland, *The Last Place on Earth*, Pan, London, 1985

Imbert, Bertrand, *North Pole, South Pole, Journeys to the Ends of the Earth*, Thames & Hudson, London, 1992

Marine Expeditions, Marine Expeditions Inc, Toronto, 1993

Mason, Anthony, *Peary and Amundsen, Race to the Poles*, Evans Brothers Ltd, London, 1995

Matthews, Rupert, *Explorer*, Dorling Kindersley, London, 1993

McGregor Dunnett, Harding, *Shackleton's Boat, The Story of the James Caird*, Neville & Harding Ltd., London

Newby, Eric, *A Book of Travellers' Tales*, Picador, London, 1986

Philips Atlas of Exploration (in association with RGS), 1996

The Photographs of HG Ponting, Discovery Limited Editions, 1996

Polar Expeditions, Expedition Advisory Centre, Royal Geographical Society, London, 1984

Rasky, Frank, *The Polar Voyagers*, McGraw-Hill Ryerson Ltd, 1976

Rootes, David, *Exploration into the Polar Regions*, Belitha Press in association with the RGS, 1994.

The Royal Geographical Society History of World Exploration, Hamlyn, London, 1991

Scott-Cowper, David, *Northwest Passage Solo*, Seafarer Books, Suffolk, 1993

Shackleton, Ernest, *South*, Robinson, London, 1998

Shackleton, Ernest, (ed) *Aurora Australis – The Book of the 1907/09 British Antarctic Expedtition* (first printed for private circulation at Cape Royds, Antarctica, 1908), Bluntisham Books & Paradigm press, Norfolk, 1986

Stroud, Mike, *Shadows on the Wasteland*, Penguin Books Ltd, London, 1994

Swallow, Sue, Hill, Christopher, *Journey Around the Arctic Circle*, Lutterworth Press, Cambridge, 1993

Thayer, Helen, *Polar Dream*, Little, Brown & Co. 1993

Unwin, Rayner, *A Winter Away From Home*, Seafarer Books, Suffolk, 1995

Usborne Geography Encyclopaedia, Usborne Publishing, London, 1998

Usborne Living World Encyclopaedia, Usborne Publishing, London,

Watt, Fiona, *The Usborne Book of the Earth*, Usborne, London, 1992

Wheeler, Sara, *Antarctica, The Falklands and South Georgia*, Cadogan Guides, London, 1997

Wheeler, Sara, *Terra Incognita*, Vintage Books, London, 1997

Worsley, Frank, A., *Shackleton's Boat Journey*, The Folio Society, London, 1974

Also, various magazines and newspapers, including *Geographical* (the magazine of The Royal Geographical Society)

The author would like to thank the following organizations for their assistance:
Royal Geographical Society, London
Expedition Advisory Centre, RGS, London
Scott Polar Research Institute, Cambridge
British Antarctic Survey, Cambridge
National Maritime Museum, Greenwich, London
Libraries in Belfast and County Down, Northern Ireland

The author would also like to thank the many individuals who have helped her and, in particular, her editor, Amanda Li.

THE JAMES CAIRD SOCIETY

If you're interested in finding out more about Sir Ernest Shackleton and his adventures, you can become a member of *The James Caird Society*.

The *James Caird* was the name of the seven-metre boat in which Shackleton and his companions made their famous 1,300 km (800 mile) journey from Elephant Island to South Georgia (see page 110). She is now preserved at Shackleton's old school, Dulwich College, in south London, though she is sometimes out on loan to exhibitions around the world.

The James Caird Society was established in 1994. It exists to preserve the memory of Sir Ernest Shackleton and to honour his remarkable feats of discovery in the Antarctic. It also remembers the qualities of leadership associated with the name of Sir Ernest Shackleton. Shackleton's granddaughter, The Hon. Alexandra Shackleton, is President of the Society.

Contact this address for further details of the society and how to join:

The Hon. Sec.
The James Caird Society
Dulwich College
London SE21 7LD

Tel: 020 8852 0302

INDEX

Numbers in bold refer to illustrations.

ACKNOWLEDGEMENTS

The author and publisher would like to thank the following for permission to include copyrighted quotations in this book:

page 2: Quotation by Dr Mike Stroud from *Shadows on the Wasteland* by Mike Stroud, published by Jonathan Cape

page 3: Quotation by David Mitchell from *GEOGRAPHICAL, THE MAGAZINE THAT EXPLORES THE WORLD*; Quotation by Apsley Cherry-Gerrard from *The Worst Journey in the World* by Apsley Cherry-Gerrard, published by Chatto & Windus

page 81: Quotation by Apsley Cherry-Gerrard from *The Worst Journey in the World* by Apsley Cherry-Gerrard, published by Chatto & Windus

page 102: Quotation by Sir Ranulph Fiennes from *Mind Over Matter* by Sir Ranulph Fiennes, published by Sinclar Stevenson

page 103: Quotation from Dr Mike Stroud from *Shadows on the Wasteland* by Mike Stroud, published by Jonathan Cape

page 110: Quotation by Commander F. A. Worsley from *Shackleton's Boat Journey*, published by The Folio Society, 1974, ©1931, The Estate of F. A. Worsley, reproduced by permission of Sheil Land Associates

Page 116: Quotation by Dick Richards, reproduced with permission of the Scott Polar Research Institute, Cambridge

page 121–122: material by Sara Wheeler precised from *Antarctica, The Falklands and South Georgia* by Sara Wheeler, published by Cadogan Guides, 1997

page 122: Quotation from Dr Mike Stroud from *Shadows on the Wasteland* by Mike Stroud, published by Jonathan Cape